Jesus & the
Forgotten
City

New Light
on Sepphoris
and the
Urban World of Jesus

Richard A. Batey

Foreword by
Paul L. Maier

Illustrated by
J. Robert Teringo

BAKER BOOK HOUSE
Grand Rapids, Michigan 49516

Jesus & the Forgotten City

To Carolyn
Light of My Life

Copyright 1991 by
Baker Book House Company

Printed in Mexico

Library of Congress Cataloging-in-Publication Data

Batey, Richard A., 1933–
    Jesus and the forgotten city : new light on the urban world of Jesus /
Richard A. Batey ; foreword by Paul L. Maier.
        p.   cm.
    Includes bibliographical references and indexes.
    ISBN 0-8010-1016-0
    1. Jesus Christ—Biography. 2. Sepphoris (Ancient city) 3. Sociology,
Urban—Israel—Galilee. I. Title.
BT303.B325   1991
232.9—dc20   91-34331
                                                                   CIP

Paintings (including cover) by J. Robert Teringo, courtesy of the National
Geographic Society.

Photographs by Jonathan Blair (pp. 27, 73); Ira Block (pp. 16–17, 21); and
Martha Cooper (pp. 23, 25, 26, 37, 57, 77, 79, 87, 91, 97, 117, 125, 139, 141,
149, 165, 169, 178). All these photographs courtesy of the National
Geographic Society.

Contents

Foreword

That more books have been written about Jesus of Nazareth than anyone who ever lived is a commonplace. The sources, however, do not permit a fully detailed biography in the modern sense, one that covers his entire life. While the culmination of Jesus' career is certainly well known, his younger years remain obscure and, barring some unforeseen discoveries, will likely remain so. Only the biblical novelist ventures any further detail on the young Jesus and his times.

The archaeological digs at Sepphoris, however, *may* change all that. This strategic city, the capital of Galilee in Jesus' youth, lay only four miles north of Nazareth, and to claim Jesus never visited the place would tax all belief, even if such visits are not specifically recorded in the New Testament. Whereas Nazareth is not mentioned in the Old Testament, and was an insignificant hamlet even in the New ("Can anything good come out of Nazareth?" Nathanael huffed), Sepphoris was "the ornament of all Galilee," according to Josephus, and the busy, bustling capital of Herod Antipas. A son of Herod the Great,

Antipas was Jesus' political sovereign, the man who executed John the Baptist and who also played a role at the trial of Jesus on Good Friday.

The Sepphoris excavations may now compel some alterations in the traditional portrait of a Jesus painted in rustic tones, a rural son of the Galilean countryside whose only urban excursion was to Jerusalem, the villager more at home in the fields and the seashore than the city. Professor Richard A. Batey finds that portrait faulty. In these intriguing pages, he overlays a fresh dimension of cosmopolitan culture onto the image of Jesus, bursting the bucolic frame that has thus far tended to delimit it. The ruins of the palace, colonnades, forum, theater, and villas at Sepphoris show that the Galilean culture affecting Jesus was far more sophisticated and urban than was previously thought possible.

Dr. Batey shows how the Sepphoris dig also sheds new light on the kind of carpentry Jesus and his foster-father Joseph pursued in Nazareth; on Jesus' use of terminology from the world of the theater in his discourses, possibly learned at the large Greco-Roman theater excavated at Sepphoris; and on how the realities of urban political life, particularly the role of kingship, intrude into Jesus' parables, a probable mirror of doings at the court of Herod Antipas.

The economy of first-century Galilee, its politics, its fiscal and taxation system, its geography, climate, commerce, highways, and many other fascinating facets that must have impinged on Jesus come into sharper focus in this book. Small wonder that he peopled his discourses with government officials, merchants, wealthy landowners, and tax collectors, not just farmers, fishermen, and shepherds. The new portrayal of Jesus emerging from these pages does not discard the familiar pastoral background so typical in the Gospels, but in adding a crucial "urban edge" to that panorama, Jesus becomes even more realistic—the savior of the city too, not just the rural redeemer.

The city not only edged dramatically into Jesus' life and ministry, but subsequently became central to the future expansion of Christianity. It was from such metropolises as Antioch, Alexandria, Ephesus, Athens, Corinth, and Rome that the faith was carried into the countryside, where the rural sorts—the *pagani* (whence the term "pagan")—were the last to convert. Thus Christianity, which began in hamlets like Bethlehem and Nazareth in the person of Jesus, finally came full circle through the mediation of urban culture.

No armchair authority, Dr. Batey is an archaeologist who has dug at Sepphoris for years, a New Testament scholar who can wield a pen as well as a spade. His extensive use of the present tense at crucial points in this book is purely intentional: the device brings the drama and color of the times quivering to life, whether describing the Battle of Actium that delivered the Roman Empire to Augustus, or the agonizing solemnities of the crucifixion at Golgotha. A lavish collection of paintings and photographs further illumines the already colorful prose, providing added delight to the reader, whether lay or professional.

I hope and trust that this book will become a standard reference work for anyone interested in the life of Jesus, as it will surely be indispensable to anyone doing research in the New Testament.

PAUL L. MAIER
Western Michigan University

Introduction

A city set on a hill cannot be hid" (Matt. 5:14). Words spoken by Jesus almost two thousand years ago spring to mind as I stand on a ridge at the edge of modern Nazareth. The hill, three miles north and seven hundred feet below, was the site of ancient Sepphoris. This beautiful Greco-Roman metropolis, adorned with colonnaded streets, forum, imposing theater, palace, and villas resplendent in white limestone and colored marble, flourished amid the forested hills and fertile valleys of northern Israel. In the decades following the birth of Jesus it was the chief city and capital of Galilee.

My view from Nazareth, one that Jesus could have seen, was described by Leroy Waterman, the University of Michigan professor who excavated at Sepphoris in 1931:

Across the rolling uplands to the north the peak of snowy Hermon hangs like a fleecy cloud above the horizon; to the west, the blue Mediterranean shimmers under the afternoon sun like a vast molten mirror, while halfway between, in full view and only an hour's walk from

Forum at Sepphoris.

Nazareth, lies the site of the city that at the beginning of the first Christian century reared its brilliant acropolis, Sepphoris, "the ornament of all Galilee," its capital and its largest and most ornate city, and at that time second only to Jerusalem in importance in all Palestine.[1]

Continuing archaeological excavations here are yielding evidence of a sophisticated urban culture that places Jesus in a radically different environment that challenges traditional assumptions about his life and ministry. The popular picture of Jesus as a rustic growing up in the relative isolation of a small village of four hundred people in the remote hills of Galilee must be integrated with the newly revealed setting of a burgeoning Greco-Roman metropolis boasting upwards of thirty thousand inhabitants—Jews, Arabs, Greeks, and Romans. Sepphoris—powerful, prosperous, peace-loving—was linked with other Greco-Roman centers on the trade routes of the Greek-speaking East.

Not that the deeply ingrained stereotype will be easily superseded. A father sought to explain to his young daughter that the familiar portrait of Jesus in white robe and halo with a lamb tucked under his arm was—in the absence of any authentic description—just an artist's conception. The little girl searched the picture, noted the lamb, the compassion in Jesus' eyes, and the serene face beneath the brownish beard. She paused, then looked up confidently. "Well, it certainly does look like him!" The new evidence being unearthed at Sepphoris is changing previous interpretations of Jesus and calls for a new appraisal of the man and the movement that he founded.

Herod Antipas, son of Herod the Great and the ruler who beheaded John the Baptist, constructed Sepphoris, after the death of his father in 4 B.C. For three decades following Jesus' birth, Sepphoris served as the capital of Galilee and Peraea, a large territory east of the Jordan River. Josephus, the first-century Jewish general and historian, whose headquarters was at Sepphoris, described the city as "the ornament of all Galilee." The proximity of Sepphoris to the satellite village, Nazareth, made contacts with this influential urban center convenient and natural.

Recently I made a tour of inspection of the acropolis at Sepphoris with professor James F. Strange, the veteran archaeologist with whom I have worked since 1980 to initiate and carry out the excavation of the ancient city. All around us rose the purposeful sounds of archaeology in action. What a contrast to the silent, abandoned acropolis overgrown with thistles and cacti my wife, Carolyn, and I had first scouted in the summer of 1979! The trenches left by Waterman's excavation had eroded and the walls had collapsed. Around the summit young pine trees planted by the Jewish National Fund were taking root among the scattered stones of the Arab village of Saffuriyye, bulldozed in the aftermath of the 1948 war. The lone structure left standing was the citadel, which had served the village as a schoolhouse and whose foundations dated to the fourth century.

When Jim Strange and I first visited the site together in 1980, it fired our interest. Two surveys of Sepphoris that we made in 1982 and 1984 served to confirm the site's potential. Clearly a city had stood here. But what were its dates, its size, its importance? Would the archaeological record support the reports by Josephus of its first-century power and grandeur?

In 1983 Jim directed the first University of South Florida excavations at Sepphoris, while I worked as the administrative director. Year after year we have returned, digging squares down through the Arab remains, to the Byzantine occupation layers, to the neatly cut Herodian-style ashlars of the Roman city, to even older levels below. Always the team kept scrupulous records of the stratigraphy as we sliced down through the layer cake of history, recording each coin and style of potsherd for computer analysis of density, distribution, and dating. No shortcuts. No treasure hunting. A solid, unassailable scientific record.

Aerial view of Sepphoris
from Nazareth.

Aerial cameras revealed walls and aqueducts; ground-penetrating radar scanned a labyrinth of tunnels, cisterns, grain silos, wine cellars, and storage chambers carved into solid rock deep below the debris of centuries. Special studies brought to light the formidable water supply system, the source of Sepphoris' pottery, the diet of the population.

The climax of our sixth season gratifyingly brought the greatest concentration to date of early first-century finds. So familiar is he with every detail of the dig, so engraved in his mind is the city plan based on hard archaeological evidence accumulated over the past years, that Jim Strange could almost walk me through the Sepphoris of Jesus' day blind-folded.

"Here was the east gate, leading toward Tiberias and Nazareth," he said. Jim was wearing his old sweat-stained leather hat and his flip-down sunglasses that protected a kind gaze from the sun's harsh glare. His full beard, streaked with gray, could not hide a warm and disarming smile that had encouraged many volunteers to work happily to the point of near exhaustion. "The wall surrounding the acropolis ran in this direction," he gestured with outstretched arms.

Walking slowly toward the afternoon sun, he pointed out main features. "The colonnaded main street, bordered by shops and public buildings, ran west to intersect the major north-south thoroughfare." On the north face of the acropolis, beyond the forum, stood excavated remains of the magnificent four-thousand-seat theater built by Herod Antipas in the early first century.

Jim continued to map out the ancient polis with its markets, pools, fountains, public baths, ritual baths (*mikvaot*), residential district, and the probable location of the royal palace of Antipas, which surely shared the design of his father's grandiose winter palace near Jericho. The fragmentary remains of mosaics, wide plaster ceiling molding, frescoed walls, nine varieties of imported marble, and

Ritual bath (*mikveh*) used for Jewish purification.

artistically crafted white building stones all witness to the opulence of this thriving city.

Although the Gospels make no specific mention of Jesus' visits to Sepphoris, the nearness of this influential urban center to its satellite village, Nazareth, made contacts easy and beneficial. There is even a tradition, first recorded in A.D. 570 by the Pilgrim of Piacenze in his *Travels,* that claims Mary's home was in Sepphoris, where she lived with her parents, Joachim and Anna, before marrying Joseph and moving to Nazareth.

Looking north from Sepphoris across the fertile fields of the Bet Netofa Valley, the breadbasket for Sepphoris, one can see the ruins of New Testament Cana six miles away, where the Gospel of John says Jesus turned water into wine at a wedding feast. Cana was also the home of the disciple Nathanael, who when told that Jesus was the Messiah, asked skeptically, "Can anything good come out of Nazareth?" (John 1:46).

The Bet Netofa Valley leads east toward the Jordan rift and the Sea of Galilee 16 miles away and 680 feet below the level of the Mediterranean. In the first century, around this beautiful blue body of fresh water teeming with fish, flourished several important towns. Near hot springs on the western shore, Antipas built another city, Tiberias, named in honor of the emperor.

My interest in Sepphoris first began in 1975, when a student at Rhodes College brought to my attention *Jesus: A New Biography,* published in 1928 by Shirley Jackson Case, professor of New Testament at the University of Chicago. Case suggested the possibility that Joseph and Jesus, both described as carpenters in the Gospels, may have worked on the extensive construction of Sepphoris less than four miles from Nazareth. Case's idea stimulated Leroy Waterman to excavate at Sepphoris for two months during the summer of 1931. Waterman clearly demonstrated that Sepphoris had been a beautiful city during Jesus' life.

Aerial view of Sepphoris, showing theater.

Research for my book *Jesus and the Poor* (1972) made me increasingly aware of the need to interpret the life and teachings of Jesus in the light of his contemporary Galilean culture. A Galilean Jew, Jesus addressed current issues of his day and responded to questions put to him by the people he encountered. A clearer grasp of the cultural environment in which Jesus lived and taught will result in a better understanding of his ministry and message. One may compare the Jesus told about in the Gospels with the cultural setting recovered from ancient texts and archaeological investigations. Sepphoris holds a key to this new understanding of Galilee and the world of Jesus.

The decision to excavate Sepphoris was cautiously made, but once determined, Carolyn and I were propelled on an adventure far greater than we had envisioned. Full-scale excavations required a highly competent archaeologist, who commanded the respect of both the Israeli Department of Antiquities as well as the American Schools of Oriental Research in the United States. That person, James F. Strange, a seasoned archaeologist, had excavated more than a decade in Israel and was a dean at the University of South Florida. Our initial survey in 1982 led the next summer to the beginning of extensive excavations at Sepphoris.

In 1985, the Joint Sepphoris Project, directed by Ehud Netzer of Hebrew University and Eric and Carol Meyers from Duke University, began to excavate at the site. Since then two separate teams have worked side by side, accelerating the recovery of this historical city. The significance of Sepphoris—a city vitally important to both Jews and Christians—is becoming increasingly apparent literally with each spade of dirt.

The central position of Sepphoris for recovering the world of Jesus has captured the attention of leading New Testament scholars. I was invited, in 1983, to present a slide lecture at a plenary session of the prestigious international society, *Studiorum Novi Testamenti Societas* (SNTS), at an

James F. Strange.

annual meeting in Canterbury. As I was concluding my address, smoke caused by a short circuit in the projector was rising at the rear of the auditorium. A sign? The lecture was warmly received and a number of enthusiastic colleagues encouraged me to continue to pursue the excavations.

During the decade of the 1980s, as the cumulative findings at Sepphoris have become increasingly exciting, it has been my privilege to chair a seminar, "Social Background of Early Christianity," at the annual meetings of *SNTS*. The cochair, Dr. Gerard Mussies of the University of Utrecht, and I have invited leading scholars to participate—scholars too numerous to mention whose names comprise an honor roll of researchers into the New Testament world. Leading these scholarly discussions over the years has profoundly informed and directed my own thinking and study and I am deeply indebted to them for their keen insights and many kindnesses.

The National Geographic Society in 1985 loaned me a ground-penetrating radar to facilitate our excavations at Sepphoris. The radar proved to be reliable in predicting subsurface features prior to excavating. Sepphoris at one time occupied approximately five hundred acres and the radar helped to focus our digging on the more promising areas.[2]

The editors of the *National Geographic* magazine realized the potentially explosive nature of the evidence being recovered at Sepphoris and its importance for a new understanding of Jesus and Christian origins. The magazine offered me a contract in August 1986 to write an article on Sepphoris and the world of Jesus. For three years I dedicated myself to drafting this article, working with gifted text editors, photographers, artists, and others. Carolyn and I traveled extensively in Europe and the Middle East, tracing out sources of relevant information. The article was completed and scheduled to appear as the lead article in the Christmas issue of 1989. Just before the presses rolled, the package was judged to be too controversial for the estimated 50 million readers of the *National*

Pottery reading on roof of Galilee Hotel in Nazareth.

Richard A. Batey operating ground-penetrating radar.

Photographing the foundations of an aqueduct.

Geographic magazine. One editor confided to me that in more than thirty years at National Geographic there had not been a firestorm to sweep through the editorial board as that ignited by the article on Sepphoris and the world of Jesus. The ideas set forth in the article have been preserved in this book, although with fuller explanations and source citations.

One significant fact has become increasingly clear from the archaeology of the past decade. Jesus lived in a Galilean culture much more urban and sophisticated than previously believed. To acknowledge this fact is to see the man and his ministry from a radically different viewpoint. Jesus in the Gospels was acquainted with the policies of kings, Antipas' government, tax collectors, wealthy land-lords, poor peasants, and actors from the theater. All these characters assume significant new roles on the stage of an urban and cosmopolitan Galilee.

More than a century ago Mark Twain stood on the shore of the Sea of Galilee on a clear night and sensed an eerie awareness of Jesus the Galilean. Twain had ridden long hot days on horseback through Syria and Palestine, depressed by the dirt and disease that he encountered in the villages. He criticized the commercialization of holy places and was characteristically cynical of the guides' spiels. But at night, camping by the sea, he felt the enchantment of the Holy Land. "In the starlight," he thought, "Galilee has no boundaries but the broad compass of the heavens, and is a theater meet for great events; meet for the birth of a religion able to save the world; and meet for the stately Figure appointed to stand upon its stage and proclaim its high decrees. . . . One can comprehend it only when night has hidden all incongruities and created a theater proper for so grand a drama."[3]

The Importance
of Sepphoris
in Jesus' Day

Now when Jesus was born in Bethlehem of
Judea in the days of Herod the king, behold,
wise men from the East came to Jerusalem,
saying, "Where is he who has been born king
of the Jews? For we have seen his star in the
East, and have come to worship him."
(Matt. 2:1–2)

Both the Gospels of Matthew (2:1) and Luke (1:5) set their stories of Jesus' birth in time and place with references to Herod the Great, whose thirty-six-year reign shaped the world into which Jesus was born. In Matthew, Herod's advisors inform him that the new king would be born in Bethlehem. The paranoid old king orders his soldiers to kill every infant under two years old in Bethlehem and the surrounding region. So it is in the Christian tradition that Herod is remembered as the king responsible for the massacre of the innocents.

The history and significance of Sepphoris in Jesus' day center on the reigns of Herod the Great and his son, Antipas, who beheaded John the Baptist. These two rulers further established Sepphoris as the seat of political power in Galilee, as was Jerusalem in the south. They forged Sepphoris into the strong central link of the chain of Greco-Roman cities in and around their realms. The amazing story of Herod's rise to power is filled with intrigue, military victories, political successes, energetic building programs, and domestic tragedies. A young man hungry for power, Herod early gained the respect and affection of the most influential figures in the Roman world—Mark Antony and Cleopatra, his mistress, Augustus, the first emperor of Rome, and Agrippa, Augustus' second in command. It was said by Herod's friends that in Augustus' affection Herod is second only to Agrippa and in Agrippa's affection Herod is second only to Augustus.[1] Herod's brilliant reign provides the background for understanding Jesus' ministry and the movement that he founded.

The Reign of Herod the Great

Our story begins in 40 B.C. with Herod, a man whose liaison with Rome's high and mighty made him a successful power broker in turbulent times. Horses at a gallop! A small band of armed men ride at break-neck speed along the coastal road leading south from Gaza toward Egypt.[2] The lead rider, Herod, glances nervously over his shoulder and leans forward in the saddle to redistribute his weight over his mount's front legs. Dust rises from the horses' hoofs. Sweat lathers on their necks and flanks. Their labored breathing signals that they cannot endure this fast pace much longer in this desperate race to freedom.

Herod wears a military officer's attire and bears a short sword at his side; a bow and quiver of arrows are strapped across the back of his saddle. A light tug on the reins slows the horses to a restful canter. The view to the right looking west is across the azure waters of the Mediterranean, shimmering with silver ripples stirred by the breeze. The rhythmic pulse of waves laps gently on the shore and foams white. Overhead sea gulls cry. To the left, in stark contrast rise the barren and forbidding hills of southern Judea and Idumea, Herod's family home— hills parched brown by the long hot summer.

Turning in his saddle, Herod surveys the road just traveled to see if his pursuers are in sight. Slowly he scans the eastern hills to detect potential threats to his passage. Finding none, he begins to assess his precarious position and plan his course of action. "I must get to Rome," he thinks. "Antony, a long-time friend of my father and our family, now has become one of the most powerful men in the Roman world. He is my best hope for support. Antony realizes the threat of the vast Parthian Empire menacing the eastern frontier of the Roman world. The Parthians have set up Antigonus as their puppet king in Jerusalem. There can be no peace for me and for Rome until Antigonus is deposed and the Parthians retreat. For the present, my family will be safe in the virtually impregnable fortress of Masada. They have adequate food and water but they cannot hold out indefinitely. I must reach Antony!"

As the day wears on the setting sun splashes bright yellows over the thin line of western clouds and conjures a golden path toward the west and Rome. As the red ball of fire extinguishes itself beneath the sea, Herod and his company arrive in the Egyptian border town of Rhinocolura.

Anxiety turns to grief. Here a messenger from Jerusalem informs Herod of his brother's fate. "The Parthians deceived Phasael and delivered him to Antigonus to be tortured. But,

Phasael cheated his tormentors. Although chained, he bashed his head against the stone wall and died." Herod knows now that his return to Judea can be only with military might.[3]

Pressing on to the port city of Pelusium on the eastern side of the Nile Delta, Herod arranges for a ship to transport him and his company to Alexandria west of the Delta. The ship glides into the famous harbor at Alexandria, one of the busiest ports on the Mediterranean; it slips past Pharos of Alexandria, a three-hundred-foot-high lighthouse built in the third century B.C. and one of the Seven Wonders of the ancient world. Here in this magnificent city Cleopatra welcomes Herod. The lavish reception in her palace precedes serious discussions of the strategy that will lay the foundation for future policies. Herod reinforces Cleopatra's fear of Parthia's threat to the lands bordering the eastern shore of the Mediterranean. So impressed is Cleopatra with Herod's commanding personality as well as his connections with Antony, that she offers him a commission in her military. Herod respectfully declines, pointing out that he must free his family besieged at Masada. He has no intention of placing himself under Cleopatra's authority.[4]

Cleopatra loans Herod a ship for his voyage to Rome. Although it is now winter and travel on the sea is very hazardous, it is a risk that Herod is compelled to take. At first, a favorable south wind speeds the ship, but after a few days the dark clouds and lashing winds of a gale-force northeaster sweep over them. Lightning bolts hurled by Zeus illumine the black sky and peals of thunder reverberate in the wooden hollow of the ship. The cargo-laden vessel rides low in the water and the huge waves wash over it, threatening to break it apart. Although seasick, the crew manages to jettison most of the cargo, all the while praying for deliverance to Poseidon, god of the sea. The howling winds wrench the ship and neither the helmsman nor the slaves manning the oars can hold her course.

With great difficulty the crew lowers a sea anchor, similar to a parachute, from the bow of the ship to hold her headed into the fierce wind. The slaves below deck draw the oars aboard and the ship rides out the violent storm. In time, the heavy seas subside, and in colder and clearer air the ship reaches the Island of Rhodes and docks in Mandraki Harbor at the City of Rhodes.

Herod prepares and equips another ship and soon continues his voyage to Rome—crossing the Aegean Sea, sailing around the southern tip of the Peloponnese, tacking north while hugging the western coast of Greece. Finally, the ship sails west across the Adriatic Sea to the port of Brundisium on the eastern shore of Italy. From Brundisium Herod hurries overland to the City of Rome.

Mark Antony, one of Rome's three triumvirs, lends an attentive ear as Herod recounts the tragic events that have brought him to Rome. Herod stresses how the Parthians, Rome's arch enemy, have installed Antigonus as their puppet king in Jerusalem. Antony recalls the hospitality and support given to him and to Julius Caesar by Herod's father, Antipater, during an earlier campaign in the East and decides that Herod is Rome's best choice for the control of Judea. In December 40 B.C., Herod and Antony walk together down the famous *Via Sacra,* the Sacred Way, where so many victorious generals had led triumphal processions and brought the world's wealth and treasures to Rome. They enter the *Curia* where the senate has assembled and Antony's spokesman begins his eloquent appeal: "I have come to praise Herod as an able leader, who has proven his loyalty to Rome." So persuasive is Antony's case for Herod, that the senate votes unanimously to appoint him king of Judea. Herod leaves the senate chamber between two of Rome's most powerful men, Antony and Octavian— men whose names will be written large on the pages of history. Octavian is the

Roman forum.

adopted son of Julius Caesar, who had been murdered only four years earlier in the senate. Destined to become Augustus, the first emperor of the Roman Empire, Octavian will become Herod's life-long patron.

Later that day Antony and Herod offer sacrifices to Capitoline Jupiter. While an owl hoots from the Palatine Hill, they celebrate their success with a lavish banquet given by Antony in Herod's honor. This is one of the most significant days in Herod's eventful career and sets in motion forces that will influence the world of Jesus. Within a week, Herod, flushed with his newly acquired kingship, braves the winter waves, sailing back to Judea to establish in fact the kingship to which he holds title.[5]

Landing at the port city of Ptolemais (present-day Akko) ten miles north of Mount Carmel, Herod conscripts an army of loyal supporters from Galilee, where he had ruled until recently as governor. Then he hastens south to Masada and liberates his family from Antigonus' threat. Herod immediately returns to Galilee and establishes a power base from which to launch a major assault on Antigonus in Jerusalem. A strategic victory in Galilee is the capture of Sepphoris, just four miles north of the little village of Nazareth. Sepphoris, a key stronghold of Antigonus, guards the intersection of major highways in the heart of Galilee.

Josephus provides the earliest written information concerning the fortified town of Sepphoris. He recounts how in 100 B.C. the king of Cyprus, Ptolemy (nicknamed Lathyrus, "chick-pea") storms Sepphoris during a campaign fought against the Jewish king Alexander Jannaeus. The defenders of Sepphoris repel Ptolemy's formidable force. Suffering heavy casualties, Ptolemy relinquishes the assault and marches to engage Alexander's army encamped on the bank of the Jordan River.[6]

Sepphoris' status and influence grow after the Roman general, Pompey, takes control of Palestine in 63 B.C. The Roman governor, Gabinius, in 55 B.C. divides the Jewish nation into five administrative districts. Sepphoris becomes the center of government for Galilee and the seat of the ruling Jewish council, the Sanhedrin.[7]

Herod knows quite well the strategic military and historical importance of Sepphoris for his conquest of Galilee. He leads a forced march against this strategic fortification in a blinding snowstorm during the winter of 39/38 B.C. Antigonus' defenders of Sepphoris flee before Herod's charge. Herod strengthens the garrison and stores weapons and provisions there, making this fortress town central for his control of all Galilee.[8]

Next Herod turns his army south, reinforced by legions sent from Antony, and rolls like a juggernaut to the gates of Jerusalem. In the late summer of 37 B.C., Jerusalem falls and a wholesale slaughter of its citizens ensues. Men, women, and children are put to the sword. Antigonus is captured, sent to Antony, and executed. Herod emerges the unrivaled king of Judea and for thirty-three years consciously shapes the destiny of his kingdom in conformity with Roman policies. But, time would not dim the memory of these atrocities perpetrated against the Holy City, nor "all the perfumes of Arabia" sweeten the hands stained by innocent Jewish blood.

The walls of Jerusalem are repaired against external threats. To counter potential rebellions within Jerusalem, Herod constructs a great fortress palace northwest of the temple precinct, naming it Antonia in honor of his patron. This fortress, 375 feet square, is similar to a fortified town, containing courts, porticoes, barracks, a parade ground, baths, and royal apartments. Four corner towers, the tallest rising more than a hundred feet, provide a commanding view of the temple courts and the city. Underground tunnels connecting the Antonia with the temple court facilitate riot control.[9] In the Antonia, Jesus will stand trial before the Roman prefect, Pontius Pilate.

From another quarter a new threat to Herod's kingship arises—a threat he is ill-equipped to fight. Cleopatra, queen of Egypt and Antony's mistress, has her eyes on Herod's rich commercial lands; Egypt borders Herod's kingdom on the south. Using her celebrated charms and probably drugs, she persuades Antony to transfer to her a coastal strip of Judea that leaves Herod virtually cut off from the Mediterranean Sea. In addition, she acquires the rich agricultural lands around Jericho north of the Dead Sea. In the vicinity of Jericho flourish lucrative date palm and balsam groves. These date palms are famous for the sweet wine produced from their fruit—a wine so potent that they are called "hang-over palms." The balsam supplies a major ingredient for the balm of Gilead, widely touted as a cure for headaches and other ailments.

After receiving these lands, Cleopatra visits Jerusalem in 34 B.C. Herod, ever the diplomat, entertains her royally

Diver at Crusader ruins.

Date palms near Jericho.

and negotiates a treaty whereby he will continue to culti-
vate the groves and will pay her the lion's share of the
profits. During this state visit, Cleopatra and Herod spend
considerable time in detailed negotiations over the future
of their two spheres of influence. Herod later claims that
Cleopatra attempted to seduce him. But Herod realizes
that this liaison could have disastrous repercussions
should word of it reach Antony. Although tempted, Herod
evades her allure and courts her only with appropriate
gifts. Then he escorts her with correct protocol to Egypt.[10]

When civil war breaks out between Antony and Octavian, a war that shakes the foundations of the Roman
Republic, Herod remains loyal to Antony and actively
supports him with troops and supplies. The decisive battle
between Octavian's navy and an armada comprised of

the combined fleets of Antony and Cleopatra is fought off the western coast of Greece near the City of Actium. This battle determines the future of the vast Roman Empire, reaching from Britain to the Persian Gulf.

At dawn on September 2, 31 B.C., the water is calm following several days of heavy seas. Antony's fleet, numbering five hundred warships, is drawn into battle formation just outside of the Ambracian Gulf, while Cleopatra's sixty huge galleys take up a protected position at the rear. Octavian's warships, although outnumbered almost two to one, are faster and more maneuverable. They are manned by experienced sailors under the expert command of Agrippa. When the battle begins, three or four of Octavian's ships surround one of Antony's larger vessels, ram it, and attack from all sides, like a pack of wolves circling a stag at bay. The rhythmic throb of the drummer quickens as he sounds the cadence for the slaves chained below deck straining at the oars. The sharp crack of the lash mingles with the order, "Full battle speed!" Then the shout, "Ramming speed! Ramming speed!" Massive bronze rams attached to the bow shatter the timbers on the sides of the enemy ship.

The command is given, "Board and give no quarter." Fully armed soldiers, spears in hand, stand poised on the deck and then leap aboard the enemy's ship as the grappling hooks are set. Men, mortally wounded, scream with their last breath and fall from the ship, staining the cool blue water with hot red blood. Fiery missiles catapulted to the lurching decks ignite ships into an inferno that will be extinguished only in their graves beneath the waves.

Dio Cassius describes the battle scene:

> Some, and particularly the sailors, perished by the smoke before the flame so much as approached them, while others were roasted in the midst of it as though in ovens. Others were consumed in their armour when it became heated. . . . Those alone found a death that was tolerable, considering the sufferings which prevailed, who were

killed by their fellows in return for the same service, or else killed themselves, before any such fate could befall them; for they not only had no tortures to endure, but when dead had the burning ships for their funeral pyres.[11]

In the heat of the battle Cleopatra gives the order and her sixty warships raise their sails and flee south toward the Peloponnese and Egypt beyond. Antony watches her flight and, deserting his brave men, sails after her. His abandoned men fight on courageously but in time surrender to Octavian. This day five thousand men lose their lives but Octavian wins the entire Roman world. Tomorrow the sea will be as yesterday, but historians will pause and ponder the prospects of this day. To commemorate this victory, Octavian builds Nikopolis, the Victory City, on the shore nearby and erects a temple honoring Neptune and Mars at the site where his command tent stood. The ruins of Nikopolis and the temple remain to this day.

The waves from this naval battle wash the shores of Judea and profoundly affect Herod's land and kingship. Word soon reaches Herod of Antony's cowardly flight from the fight at Actium and of the surrender of his forces to Octavian. This news casts a dark cloud over Herod's future, but he is determined to confront Octavian face to face and sue for peace. In the spring of 30 B.C., Octavian travels to the Island of Rhodes to prepare his invasion of Egypt.

Herod sails to Rhodes to discover his fate. Before being admitted to Octavian's presence, Herod lays aside his royal crown but assumes a regal bearing. Standing before Octavian, Herod reviews his enthusiastic and loyal support of Antony both before and during the tragic civil war and concludes his appeal, acknowledging, "I share Antony's defeat and with his downfall lay down my diadem. I am come to you resting my hope of safety upon my integrity, and presuming that the subject of inquiry

Sunrise at Mandraki Harbor, Rhodes.

will be not whose friend, but how loyal a friend I have been." Octavian, well aware of the indispensable support that Herod could provide in the upcoming campaign against Egypt, reaffirms Herod's kingship over Judea and promises even larger benefits that will replace the loss of Antony's patronage.[12] As Herod sails from Mandraki Harbor toward Judea, the sunrise greets him; at Rhodes, the island of the sun, a new day has dawned on Herod's illustrious career.

In late summer, Octavian arrives with his army at Ptolemais, the port city on the northern border of Herod's kingdom. Herod welcomes Octavian and rides beside him while Octavian reviews his troops. Herod quarters Octavian and his officers in opulent apartments specially prepared for their visit and lavishly entertains them. Then Herod escorts Octavian and his army the entire length of Judea to the border of Egypt, and provides them with an abundant supply of food, water, and wine.[13]

This journey gives Octavian the opportunity to inspect Herod's kingdom and to give directives for future policies that will preoccupy Herod's long rule and shape the world of Jesus. Herod must strengthen his kingdom as a buffer state against the threats of the Parthians to the east and the Arabs to the southeast. A ring of massive fortresses must be constructed or strengthened to contain these enemies. To develop a vital economy and flourishing trade a major port city will need to be built. This port will provide for the easy transport of both goods and military materiel. Herod will need a fierce secret police to keep a watchful eye on the people and to preserve internal security. Roman culture must pervade Herod's kingdom as it reflects Roman style and values. By the time Herod and Octavian reach the border of Egypt, Herod has no doubts as to his kingly responsibilities.

After Octavian conquers Egypt and Antony and Cleopatra have committed suicide, Herod goes to Egypt to congratulate Octavian on his victory. Octavian returns Herod's lands that Antony had given to Cleopatra and in addition gives Herod several important cities. Octavian also makes a special gift of Cleopatra's elite bodyguard, comprised of four hundred fierce Gauls. Herod escorts Octavian on his long march from Egypt to Antioch in Syria and strengthens their bond of friendship. From this time forward, Herod exemplifies an unswerving loyalty to Octavian and to Rome.

Herod strengthens existing fortresses and builds new ones along the borders of Judea—Masada, Cyprus, two Herodiums (one east, one west of the Jordan River), Hyrcania, Alexandrium, and Machaerus. Located on mountain peaks, these fortresses could communicate at night with fire signals. Specially trained carrier pigeons guarantee same-day delivery of important messages.[14]

Through numerous Roman importations and grandiose building projects, Herod's kingdom mirrors Augustan Rome. He renovates the Holy City and creates the ambi-

Herod's tombs of the patriarchs in Hebron.

ence with which Jesus would be familiar. Herod chooses Jerusalem, the capital of his kingdom, for his most daring innovations. In 28 or 27 B.C. he celebrates the first Actium Games, held every four years, in honor of Octavian's naval victory over Antony and Cleopatra. (Herod also sends an extravagant donation to help pay for the construction of Nikopolis, Octavian's "Victory City.") To celebrate the games in grand style, Herod undertakes an aggressive building program at Jerusalem. Just south of the temple mount he builds a large hippodrome where chariot races—both two- and four-horse—thrill vast crowds. There are also horse races, the jockeys whipping their mounts around the course, vying for generous purses.[15]

Outside the city wall Herod constructs two additional

buildings, a theater and an amphitheater (an oval-shaped arena). In the latter trained gladiators fight to the death before excited, blood-thirsty mobs. Wild animals, many imported from Africa, are pitted against one another in mortal combat. Slaves and condemned prisoners fight with wild beasts while spectators place their bets and cheer their favorites. Most Jews are incensed by these gory spectacles in which human life is sacrificed for public entertainment, but some attend, desiring to be fashionable as well as enjoying the cruelty.[16]

Gymnastic competitions also comprise an essential part of the games—foot races, discus throw, boxing, high jump, broad jump, javelin throw, and wrestling. Herod prides himself on being physically strong, agile, and skilled with weapons of war—sword, bow and arrow, and javelin. To entice the best athletes, he offers huge prizes to the winners and circulates the announcement to lands far and wide. The nudity of the Greek-style athletes is yet another affront to Jewish sensibilities. The athletes wear distinctive hats as they stride through the streets of Jerusalem—but only hats.

To further impress the crowds that throng to Jerusalem for the games—for a major concern is to win the approval of tourists—Herod builds a zoo that houses exotic animals. These animals, selected for their enormous strength or rarity, are placed on public display; some will fight in the amphitheater.[17]

Herod is also an entrepreneur. Superior athletes and acclaimed artists attend his games as well as the most famous celebrities, royalty, and influential people from foreign lands. He organizes a trade fair to show off serviceable objects—in part military equipment—the latest fashions, and gold and silver vessels inlaid with costly jewels. This exhibition helps to stimulate trade and to balance his budget.[18]

The grand theater, erected south of the city, is lavish in its design and exhibits stone inscriptions honoring Octavian and recounting his great exploits. A Roman theater customarily would be decorated with marble statues. But, because of the second commandment proscribing graven images, Herod adorns his theater with trophies, armor captured in battle. These suits of armor made of pure silver or gold are a fitting tribute to the king's own military prowess.

In this elaborate theater competitions are held in music, drama, and oratory. Herod assures the highest quality of professionalism in the performing arts by bestowing both glory and munificent awards on the winners. The most celebrated artists attend these galas and are treated to luxurious accommodations. "And whatever costly or magnificent efforts had been made by others, all these did Herod imitate in his ambition to see his spectacle become famous," wrote Josephus.[19]

Many resident Jews take pleasure in the performances in the theater. But the more scrupulous suspect that the gold and silver armor hides statues and complain bitterly until one of the trophies is dismantled. To their chagrin only the bare wooden frame stands beneath.[20]

Herod is an avid promoter of his theater and frequently attends the productions. Some Jews, who deeply resent Herod's Idumean ancestry and his leaning over backward to please Rome, conspire to kill him in his theater. They consider this controversial theater the appropriate stage upon which to bring down the final curtain on Herod's despised reign. Just as Herod is entering the theater, however, their plot is discovered and the would-be-assassins are arrested, tortured, and executed.[21]

Two additional Herodian structures, the citadel and the temple, dominate the skyline of Jerusalem. In 23 B.C. construction begins on the citadel, Herod's monumental palace twice the size of the Antonia. Erected on the western ridge of the Upper City, the citadel guards the Jaffa Gate. The palace's forty-five-foot-high wall of cut stone boasts three massive towers. The tallest, soaring to a

Herod's citadel in Jerusalem.

height of 128 feet, provides visual communication with the fortresses to the south. This royal residence, a city within a city, is the administrative center of Herod's kingdom. The main palace, surrounded by verdant lawns and trees watered by fountains and pools, is a paragon of oriental extravagances. The royal apartments, with imported marble walls and huge carved cedar ceiling beams, are appointed with sculptures, paintings, and furnishings of gold and silver. Two cavernous halls, named appropriately Augustus and Agrippa, are each ample enough to sleep a hundred guests.[22]

The crowning architectural achievement of Herod's Jerusalem is the temple. Construction begins in 20 B.C., the same year that Octavian, now the emperor Augustus, comes to Antioch in Syria. Herod visits Augustus in Antioch and discusses the delicate political implications of constructing in Jerusalem a magnificent temple to the exclusively Jewish God. Herod plans for the temple to be the centerpiece of his extensive urban renewal projects and hopes that it will help to ingratiate him with his estranged Jewish subjects. He also realizes the economic advantages of the temple, which will bring vast revenues to Jerusalem from the numerous pilgrims celebrating the annual holy festivals.

The new temple is erected on the east side of Jerusalem on the site where Solomon's temple originally stood. The area of the temple mount is virtually doubled by substructures built into the hillside and paved with large smooth stones. Surrounding this approximately thirty-five-acre pavement, called the Court of the Gentiles, is a magnificent colonnade of beautiful Corinthian columns. When Jesus drives the money changers and those selling sacrificial animals from the temple, it is from this court.

Ten thousand workmen, masons, and carpenters are engaged in the massive construction—some employed on the site, others in the deep quarries cutting gigantic blocks of the famous Jerusalem stone with its subtle golden hue. Of these huge ashlars Jesus' disciples will observe, "Look, Teacher, what wonderful stones and what wonderful buildings!" (Mark 13:1). Herod's architects and workers complete the construction of the temple sanctuary in only eighteen months, but work continues on the temple precinct for many years.[23]

In 15 B.C., Agrippa, second to Augustus in power, pays a state visit to Judea accompanied by his wife Julia, the promiscuous daughter of Augustus. Herod provides the couple with a royal tour of his defenses and his other grand building projects. When they arrive in Jerusalem, Herod lodges his guests in the royal apartments of his new palace. Agrippa responds by giving sumptuous

Western wall of the temple built by Herod the Great.

banquets at which toasts and compliments are affectionately exchanged. Agrippa visits the temple and has one hundred oxen sacrificed on the high altar. Even a gate of the temple is named in his honor. As Herod escorts Agrippa to his ship docked at Caesarea, he could rest assured that his beautiful temple pleased both Rome and the Jews.[24]

When Agrippa sails from Caesarea, the magnificent harbor begun in 22 B.C. is nearing completion. This harbor provides Judea with a major port and grants access to Rome's maritime trade. Additionally, it serves as a depot for Roman military supplies, necessary for Rome's defense against the Parthians. The harbor is the largest man-made anchorage to be constructed up until this time. Advanced design and innovative technology are employed to counter the effects of the

strong south-north current—heavily laden with sand from Egypt and the Sinai—and the relentless pounding of the surf. The remains of hydraulic concrete, poured under water, testify to the sophistication of the Roman engineers. One slab measures 45 x 33 x 6 feet.[25]

The harbor at Caesarea, the first truly modern harbor, is both functional and beautiful. The six-hundred-yard-long south breakwater and the three-hundred-yard-long north breakwater are lined with warehouses. A tall lighthouse guards the entrance from the north; smoke and flame guide merchantmen safely to port. Statues adorning the approach welcome sailors to the gateway of Herod's kingdom. A majestic temple dedicated to Augustus and Rome dominates the view eastward.[26]

The city itself, laid out on the Roman grid plan, contains architecture typical of a great Roman city—colonnaded main street, theater, hippodrome, public baths, and administrative buildings.

Herod's navy, built of timber felled on the forested slopes above Caesarea, plies the sea lanes and imports great riches. Judea exported walnuts, flax, date palm syrup, balsam, and slaves. Herod spends many months at sea maintaining contacts with powerful people, personally managing foreign policy, and negotiating lucrative business contracts. One such deal is struck with the emperor himself; in 12 B.C. Herod pays Augustus three hundred talents for half the revenues received from the Cyprus copper mines—mines so productive that they supply markets all the way to India.

In addition to the merchantmen, the navy includes a formidable fleet of warships that protect Herod's commercial interest. This navy Herod also uses to assist in preserving the *Pax Romana*. In 14 B.C. he sails his flagship, leading a fleet of warships, to Sinope on the southern shore of the Black Sea to assist Agrippa in putting down a rebellion.[27]

Generous gifts to neighboring cities enhance Herod's growing international reputation. Athens and major Greek cities bordering on the Aegean Sea are the special recipients of his munificence. The Greeks held Herod in such high esteem that they selected him to be the honorary president of the Olympic Games.

With the advance of years, Herod's vitality wanes. His wives—he had married ten—and their sons vie for power. Attempts on Herod's life feed a growing suspicion. A recurring nightmare of his assassination at the hand of one of his sons haunts his dreams. He has some of his sons put to death on rather flimsy circumstantial evidence. When the report of Herod's seemingly irrational behavior reaches Augustus, he turns it aside with the pun roughly translated, "I would rather be Herod's sow than

Herodium—Herod's burial site.

son." (Herod observed the Jewish prohibition against eating pork.)

Prior to Herod's death in the spring of 4 B.C., he is very sick and in great pain. He fears, with good reason, that his death will be the occasion for great celebration. To insure that the kingdom will be filled with loud lamentations, he summons highly respected Jews from throughout his realm to assemble in the hippodrome at Jericho. When they arrive, he has them arrested and held in detention until after his death. He gives his guards the order to murder them immediately following his death. After Herod dies the order is ignored.[28]

Herod's lavish funeral is a tribute to the achievements of his illustrious thirty-six-year reign. His body—dressed in royal robes, crowned, and still holding his scepter—is borne on a solid gold bier. The funeral procession, comprised of family members, bodyguard, and a regiment of the army, winds its way slowly to the Herodium south of Jerusalem. Here in a secret tomb Herod is buried.[29] At last, easy rests the head that wore the crown.

Division of Herod's Kingdom

Following the death of Herod the Great, his kingdom is divided, as stipulated in his final will, among three of his sons. Antipas inherits Galilee and Peraea and receives the title of "tetrarch," signifying the ruler of one-fourth of a kingdom. Archelaus, the older full brother of Antipas, becomes the ruler of Judea and Samaria, receiving the more important title of "ethnarch," meaning "ruler of a nation." Philip, Herod's son by his wife Cleopatra of Jerusalem, becomes tetrarch of the territories northeast of the Sea of Galilee.[30]

Before the sons can assume power, Augustus has to ratify Herod's will. Antipas is sixteen years old and Archelaus eighteen when in May 4 B.C., they sail on separate ships from Caesarea to Rome. Each is accompanied by royal family members and legal council. Antipas and Archelaus both had received their educations in Rome. In fact, when Antipas arrives back in Rome in mid-summer, he has been gone from Rome about six months. Lawyers representing Antipas and Archelaus contest Herod's will in the imperial court until early fall. Then Philip arrives with his own delegation. After the summations are eloquently presented to Augustus, he makes the decision to honor Herod's last will virtually as written.

The three sons spend the winter in Rome and return to Judea in the spring of 3 B.C. to take charge of their lands and people. This time in Rome provides Antipas, now officially tetrarch of Galilee and Peraea, an opportunity to obtain expert advice and to formulate specific plans concerning the establishment of his government and the building of his capital.[31]

Following Herod's death, riots and rebellions flare up in several places throughout his kingdom. A center of the uprisings in Galilee is Sepphoris, where a rebel leader named Judas the son of Ezechias, attacks Herod's arsenal and arms his men with weapons stored there. The people of Sepphoris are unwilling or perhaps unable to prevent his rebellion. Judas' rash action prompts the Roman legate of Syria, Quintilius Varus, to order his legions to crush the rebels in Galilee. The Roman army, commanded by Varus' son and Gaius, a friend of Varus, is supported by infantry and cavalry sent by Aretas, king of Arabia. This combined force attacks Sepphoris, captures and burns the city, and sells the inhabitants into slavery.[32] Varus, as a matter of routine, would report and justify to the emperor significant troop movement and battles, especially a battle as important as the destruction of Sepphoris. Such vital information received in the imperial court naturally would be conveyed to Antipas, since it directly involved his sphere of authority and responsibility.

When Antipas returns to Galilee from Rome in the spring of 3 B.C., he selects the smoldering ruins of Sepphoris for the location of his new capital. Centrally situated in Galilee, Sepphoris had a long and impressive history as a seat of government. Antipas launches a vast construction project that lasts throughout the life of Jesus, who was born about 6 B.C. Sepphoris becomes the nerve center for the government's control of Galilee and Peraea. Political policy, military strategy, economic regulations, and cultural affairs will be administered from this seat of power. Influences from Sepphoris affect the people living in Nazareth and other satellite villages. Josephus describes Sepphoris as the largest and most beautiful city in the region.[33]

J. ROBERT TERINGO

Artist's reconstruction
of the acropolis at Sepphoris.

One may envision Antipas riding on his swift Arabian stallion to the crest of the Sepphoris hill, escorted by his elite horse guard. Accompanying Antipas are architects, engineers, and city planners like those who recently built Caesarea Maritima, Sebaste, the Jerusalem temple, and Herod's palaces in Jerusalem and Jericho. They pause among the ashes and broken walls on the summit to survey the landscape. To the north the broad and rich Bet Netofa Valley is green from the spring rains. The valley stretches from the Mediterranean Sea east toward the Jordan Rift and the Sea of Galilee. Verdant forests cover the surrounding hills. Mount Carmel, eighteen miles to the west, juts into the Mediterranean. The high ridge to the south hides from view the village of Nazareth nestled around its pleasant spring.

The city plan, laid out on the Roman grid pattern adjusted to the contours of the land, has all those constructions typical of a splendid Roman provincial capital—a main east-west street leading to the forum, Antipas' royal residence with its imposing tower that offers a breathtaking panorama, a four-thousand-seat theater, bath, bank, archives, gymnasium, basilica, water works, and other buildings.

Serving resident high-ranking Roman officials there will be a temple dedicated to Augustus and to Rome, modeled on those temples built by Herod the Great at Caesarea and Sebaste. The new capital is named *Autocratoris,* the Greek equivalent of the Latin *Imperator,* a title given to Augustus meaning "commander-in-chief." Herod the Great had named the port city Caesarea Maritima in honor of Augustus and had called the fortress city of Samaria by the new name "Sebaste," the Greek translation of Augustus. Herod's son Philip would soon lay the foundation of his capital and call it Caesarea Philippi. Antipas with Herodian political astuteness also names his capital in honor of the Roman emperor.[34]

Gentile cultic objects from Sepphoris.

An Introduction to Herod Antipas

Who is this young ruler, who builds his beautiful capital four miles north of Jesus' home in Nazareth? Who rules Galilee and Peraea for more than four decades. Who beheads John the Baptist. Who attempts unsuccessfully to arrest Jesus but does interrogate him during the trial before his crucifixion.

Antipas, the second son of Herod the Great and his second wife, Malthace, is born about 20 B.C.—the same year that Herod began construction on the Jerusalem temple. Born to the purple, Antipas enjoys the privileges of princely rank in the luxury of the royal household. As a potential heir to the throne his education is of primary importance. In addition to instruction in Hebrew and Jewish law and religious practices, he takes studies that prepare him for advanced training in Rome.

Herod ships Antipas off to Rome at the tender age of twelve to prepare to become king. For three years Antipas receives the best education that Rome has to offer. Herod also had sent his other sons to Rome for their education. Responsibility for Antipas' instruction in Roman culture falls to a highly respected man of letters named Pollio, probably Asinius Pollio, a celebrated historian, poet, and orator, who reputedly is a friend of the Jews.[35]

The long and close friendship between Antipas' father and the emperor grants a special status to the young prince among persons of influence in Rome. It is an exciting time for a young man of privilege. As Antipas strolls through the Eternal City, he sees on all sides concrete signs that the Golden Age of Augustus has fully dawned.

Architecture recites history. An initial orientation to Augustan Rome introduces Antipas to significant buildings and monuments that reflect the city's past and values. Sources do not recount the details of Antipas' education, but much is known about the Rome that Antipas encountered when he arrived in 8 B.C. It is possible through historical research to conjure the Rome that Antipas knew.

A visitor to Augustan Rome in 8 B.C. might begin a tour at the center of the Roman Forum as the morning sun streams through the three high vaults of the Arch of Augustus. This massive triumphal arch, erected soon after the Battle of Actium, commemorates Octavian's naval victory over Antony and Cleopatra.[36] Beyond the arch stands the small round Temple of Vesta, where the Vestal Virgins tend the sacred fire, symbolizing the life of the City of Rome.[37] To the left is the Temple of Julius Caesar, who had adopted Octavian and made him his heir. From its beautiful porch Mark Antony had given Julius Caesar's funeral oration.[38]

Walking along the *Via Sacra* (Sacred Way), one passes the *Curia* (senate house) where thirty-two years earlier the senate had named Antipas' father king of Judea. Leaving the Roman Forum one strolls past the Forum of Julius Caesar and soon arrives at the magnificent Forum of Augustus, where construction begun more than three decades earlier continues.[39] Three hundred yards west is the Campidoglio, where Augustus had rebuilt the ancient Temple of Jupiter Optimus Maximus as an initial phase of an extensive urban renewal program.

A short distance north on the *Via Lata* is the *Ara Pacis,* the altar of Augustan Peace, commissioned by the senate to celebrate Augustus' military victories over the Gauls and Spain. Enclosed within a quadrangle of white marble, the altar displays the pious imperial family in a sacrificial procession. Among the figures carved from the marble stands Agrippa, Augustus' second in command, who visited Jerusalem when Antipas was only five years old.[40] Not far west of the *Ara Pacis* flows the Tiber River. On its east bank Augustus has built his imposing mausoleum, a magnificent circular tomb measuring 300 feet in diameter and rising to a height of 137 feet. Atop the

Statue of Augustus,
Vatican Museum.

mausoleum stands a large gilt bronze statue of Augustus. At the tomb's entrance stands two tall pink granite obelisks to which are attached bronze tablets recording the *Res Gestae,* Augustus' great works and accomplishments. But, alas all earthly glories pass.[41] South along the graceful bends in the river one comes on the 15,000-seat Theater of Marcellus, dedicated by Augustus three years earlier in honor of his nephew. The brilliant design of its facade will in time inspire Renaissance architecture but at

Augustus' mausoleum.

present it is a vivid reminder that Augustus is an avid benefactor of the performing arts.[42]

Turning east one soon begins to ascend the southwest slope of the Palatine Hill, one of seven hills on which Rome was built. From this vantage point it is possible to look down on the Circus Maximus, a long narrow racecourse capable of seating 250,000 spectators.[43] On the Palatine, where Augustus had been born fifty-five years before, he has erected an imperial residence befitting the ruler of the world. Nearby he constructed an awe-inspiring Temple of Apollo to honor the god of light and reason. Next to the temple Augustus built a magnificent library, a focal point of learning and culture for the envisioned golden age. Manuscript copies of classical Greek and Roman thinkers as well as outstanding contempo-

Roman sacrificial procession.

rary men of letters are preserved here. This certainly is a place with which Antipas will become familiar.[44]

For three years Antipas pursues his education under the watchful care of distinguished teachers. It is essential that this royal prince, named in Herod's fifth will as the sole heir of the Kingdom of Judea, be familiar with Roman judicial policy and statesmanship. Antipas' subsequent long and peaceful reign suggests that he learned his lessons well. Late in 5 B.C. his studies are interrupted by the disturbing news that his father is seriously ill and the physicians do not think that he can live much longer. The message, imprinted with Herod's own seal, concludes with the summons, "Antipas come home with all haste. Your father wishes to see you while there is yet time."

Arriving in Judea, Antipas finds his father in increasing pain and deteriorating physical and mental health. Herod confers with Antipas, whom he had not seen since Antipas sailed to Rome at age twelve, and decides that Antipas is not yet ready to rule over all the Kingdom of Judea. A short time before his death Herod adds a codicil to his will reducing Antipas' territories to Galilee and Peraea. Once Augustus ratifies this final will, Antipas is prepared to take control and build a powerful and prosperous realm with a brilliant new Roman-style capital city, Sepphoris.[45] This large and ongoing construction directly influences life in the whole region—especially in the nearby villages like Nazareth.

Jesus the Carpenter

Many who heard [Jesus] were astonished, saying, "Where did this man get all this? What is the wisdom given to him? What mighty works are wrought by his hands! Is not this the carpenter, the son of Mary and brother of James and Joses and Judas and Simon, and are not his sisters here with us?" (Mark 6:2–3)

Jesus is described once in the New Testament as a carpenter (Mark 6:3) and once as "the carpenter's son" (Matt. 13:55).[1] Nothing more is said about his occupation. An occupation expresses an essential aspect of a person's life, providing a setting for daily associations that profoundly influence one's language, social standing, and economic status. At work attitudes are frequently formed concerning the use of money, political policies, moral values, and even religious faith. A fuller understanding of Jesus' work promises a better understanding of the man and the movement that he founded.

Popular piety has provided a picture of Jesus working as a young apprentice in his father Joseph's carpenter shop. The romanticized scene is familiar. The young Jesus, with muscular arms and calloused hands, helps Joseph in their little Nazareth carpenter shop. But, significant new evidence surfacing in the excavations at Sepphoris is casting fresh light on the carpenter's trade in the vicinity of Nazareth. We will first sketch the traditional vignette of Joseph's carpenter shop, and then explore the revised understanding of Jesus' occupation required by the realization that he grew up within sight of a burgeoning new Greco-Roman capital city.

Traditional View of Jesus' Occupation

Joseph's shop is usually imagined to be in the courtyard of his small house in Nazareth. Closing off one side of the courtyard is a shed with double doors opened to reveal a sturdy oak workbench that can be moved outside during the long dry season. Inside the shed, stacked in neat piles, are rough planks of different local woods—oak, pine, cypress, and sycamore fig. For special projects, such as furniture and kitchen utensils, there is walnut, cedar, and olive wood.

The hand tools—similar to those from the Roman period discovered by archaeologists or that survive on reliefs—are scattered over the work bench and hang on the wall of the shed. Most of these tools would be familiar to present-day carpenters. To lay out the design there is a ruler, a square, straightedge, chalkline, plumbline, level, and marker or scriber.

Against the shed leans an ax to fell select trees for timber from the nearby forest. On the wall hangs a large saw for ripping boards. In the firm grip of the carpenter's strong hands, hatchet, mallet and chisel, plane, knife, and adze fashion the wood to his will. For drilling holes, there is a bow drill that has a leather thong looped around a sharp iron drill. With one hand the carpenter moves the bow back and forth, making the drill spin first in one direction and then the other. With his other hand he holds the drill firmly in place by a wooden cap on its top. Wooden dowel pins driven into the smooth holes hold the joints tightly together. The carpenter employs an awl or gimlet to drill smaller holes and hammers in iron nails. This prevents the nails from bending and the wood from splitting.

A lathe holds a two-inch-square stick of walnut about two feet long. Iron pins have been inserted into holes drilled in the center of each end of the stick. Again a bow with a leather thong looped around the stick is pulled back and forth to make the stick rotate, while a sharp chisel is held gently but firmly against it. Soon the spinning stick of walnut is transformed into a spindle for a fine chair.

A carpenter in Nazareth manufactures a variety of items for the local market. Basic household furniture includes tables, chairs and stools, beds, lamp stands, and storage chests. Farm implements made for peasants and tenant farmers are plows, threshing boards, winnowing forks, yokes for oxen, and even carts and wagons. With simple hand tools a skilled carpenter, a chip of wood tucked behind his ear as a sign of his trade, can produce quality products.[2]

The construction of village houses requires the carpenter's craftsmanship to cut trees and hew ceiling beams. Doors and frames for doors and windows must be built strong and square. Occasionally the carpenter contracts with a prosperous farmer to build "a bigger and better barn" in which to store a bumper crop.[3]

J. ROBERT TERINGO

Construction
of Sepphoris.

Revised Understanding of Jesus' Occupation

This traditional scene of Joseph and Jesus working as carpenters in Nazareth must now be reexamined, keeping in mind the archaeological evidence unearthed at Sepphoris—evidence that places Jesus' early years in an entirely different cultural environment. In 3 B.C., when Jesus is about three years old, Herod Antipas chooses Sepphoris as the site for his new capital of both Galilee and Peraea. For more than three decades while Jesus grows up in nearby Nazareth a huge construction project continues, as Sepphoris rapidly becomes the largest and most influential city in the region. The city's inhabitants, soon numbering almost thirty thousand, are sophisticated and cosmopolitan Jews, Arabs, Greeks, and Romans.

A ten-minute walk from the Nazareth spring to the top of the ridge north of the village rewards one with the magnificent vista of the broad and fertile Bet Netofa Valley a thousand feet below. The hill of Sepphoris, three miles north, rises almost four hundred feet from the valley floor. This is a beautiful and inviting view toward the site of ancient Sepphoris.

Joseph and Jesus knew of the construction of the new capital and would have been acquainted with artisans and other workers employed on the site. Shirley Jackson Case, professor of New Testament at the University of Chicago, made a fascinating observation based on his reading of Josephus, the first-century Jewish historian who knew Sepphoris well. "Very likely 'carpenter' as applied to Jesus meant not simply a worker in wood but one who labored at the building-trade in general, and it requires no very daring flight of the imagination to picture the youthful Jesus seeking and finding employment in the neighboring city of Sepphoris. But whether or not he actually labored there, his presence in the city on various occasions can scarcely be doubted; and the fact of such contacts during the formative years of his young man-hood may account for attitudes and opinions that show themselves conspicuously during his public ministry."[4]

Visits of Jesus to Sepphoris are not recorded by the Gospel writers, who give only fragmentary accounts of his life and ministry. After Jesus became widely recognized as an influential religious leader, Antipas sought to arrest him. Sepphoris would not be a safe setting in which to proclaim the coming kingdom of God. The Gospels do tell of Jesus' travels throughout all the cities and villages of Galilee and into Phoenicia, Caesarea Philippi, and the Decapolis, as well as journeys through Samaria to Jerusalem in Judea. It is difficult to believe that, during the approximately thirty years that Jesus grew up looking at Sepphoris, he never visited the capital or met the people living and working there. Even casual contacts with the capital would have given Jesus firsthand knowledge of Greco-Roman city planning, architectural design, and sophisticated engineering technology—as well as the cosmopolitan citizens.

The walk from Nazareth to Sepphoris takes about an hour. I had driven the distance between Nazareth and the excavations at Sepphoris over four hundred times, but in the summer of 1988 I took the opportunity to walk. I awoke at four A.M., dressed hurriedly, and forced down a breakfast of hot coffee and dry bread spread with jam and peanut butter. When the bus carried the diggers to the excavation at 4:30 A.M., it was still dark. A few minutes later when I left the Galilee Hotel, our home in the center of old Nazareth, the first light of dawn outlined the eastern hills. As I walked toward Mary's Well, the spring of ancient Nazareth, the streets were empty—a sharp contrast to the noise and stifling fumes of the daytime traffic. Here and there I encountered an industrious merchant up early preparing to open his shop. We did not exchange greetings in the darkness.

By the time I reached the top of the ridge the sun greeted me and cast its soft amber rays over the low-lying, blue-gray mist in the valley below. Somehow on foot the familiar panorama seemed even more peaceful and inviting. Looking toward the hill of Sepphoris, I recalled again Jesus' words, "A city set on a hill cannot be hid" (Matt. 5:14). Strolling down the north side of the ridge and across the gently rolling hills toward Sepphoris, I became keenly aware of the ease with which traffic moved between Nazareth and Sepphoris and wondered how often Jesus may have walked this way.

Sepphoris provides a significant new perspective for understanding the world in which Jesus lived and worked, both as a carpenter and religious teacher. The construction of Antipas' Sepphoris viewed from the ridge above Nazareth is reminiscent of a scene from Virgil's epic poem, *The Aeneid*—a passage that Antipas probably read during his studies in Rome. Aeneas, the legendary founder of Rome, and his companion, climb to the brow of a hill that overlooks the building of the City of Carthage. Located on the North African coast near present-day Tunis, Carthage had rivaled Rome's expansion in the Mediterranean. It is interesting that the Phoenician city of Tyre, less than forty miles north of Sepphoris, had founded Carthage as an important colony for their trading empire. The scene of Carthage's construction is compared by Virgil to a hive of activity: "Even as bees in early summer, amid flowery fields, ply their task in sunshine."

Virgil describes Carthage's vast building project and points out the major urban installations and facilities:

> And now they were climbing the hill that looms large over the city and looks down on the confronting towers. Aeneas marvels at the massive buildings, mere huts once; marvels at the gates, the din and paved high-roads. Eagerly the Tyrians press on, some to build walls, to rear the citadel, and roll up stones by hand; some to choose the site for a

James F. Strange and model of the acropolis at Sepphoris.

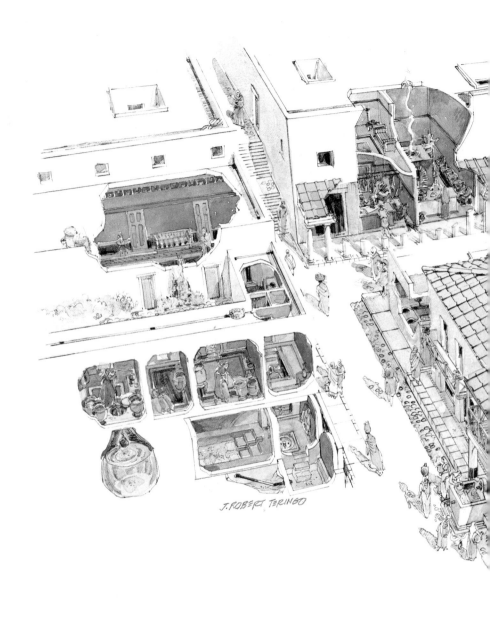

First-century Roman
apartment house.

dwelling and enclose it with a furrow. Laws and magistrates they ordain, and a holy senate. Here some are digging harbours, here others lay the deep foundations of their theatre and hew out of the cliffs vast columns, lofty adornments for the stage to be![5]

The construction of an influential Roman capital city near Jesus' home in Nazareth redefines the carpenter's occupation in central Galilee. In 4 B.C. Varus' army crushed the rebellion centered at Sepphoris, burned the old town, and sold the inhabitants into slavery. To erect Antipas' new capital, many skilled workers from surrounding towns and villages came to Sepphoris and found employment. Artisans from Nazareth would have been among those employed.

The Greek word *tektōn,* translated "carpenter" in Mark 6:3, has the root meaning of "artisan," that is, a skilled worker who works on some hard material such as wood or stone or even horn or ivory. A metal smith also might be described as a *tektōn.* The preferred translation of *tektōn* in Mark 6:3 is "carpenter." In Jesus' day construction workers were not as highly specialized as in today's work force. For example, the tasks performed by carpenters and masons could easily overlap. When a *tektōn,* or artisan, from a village near Sepphoris, visited the construction site, he would be introduced to another world—an urban world.[6]

Construction at Sepphoris

Combining information from ancient writers with the new scientific evidence unearthed at Sepphoris, it is possible to recreate the life of this burgeoning capital.[7] A visitor from Nazareth to Antipas' Sepphoris approaches from the east along a low ridge. The road follows close beside the new covered aqueduct bringing fresh spring water from

Reservoir at Sepphoris.

Abel three miles east of the city. A mile east of Sepphoris is a huge underground reservoir with a capacity of approximately one million gallons. A natural limestone cave has been sealed with hydraulic plaster to form a one-hundred-yard-long underground lake. At the west end of the reservoir a tunnel leads to a water gate that regulates the flow of water to the city through the aqueduct. Near the outer city wall are a pair of sediment pools used to settle out deposits suspended in the water. One pool can be cleaned without shutting off the city's water supply. Beyond the pools arches carry the aqueduct across a shallow valley to a large pool on the side of the hill of the acropolis. From this pool, waterwheels powered by slaves lift the water to stepped pools and gardens on top of the acropolis. Water flowing from one pool to another finally fills large plastered cisterns carved into the soft rock of the acropolis.[8]

Close to the east gate of the city the road widens into a broad plaza where local farmers sell their produce—beans, cucumbers, melons, olives, and lentils. The city gates, flanked by two tall square towers, permit the easy flow of traffic, while soldiers posted on the flat roofs casually survey the scene below. Other guards patrol the top of the wall between similar towers built at regular intervals. Through the gate a wide paved street ascends to the acropolis. Crowds throng the street as people jostle one another, intently pursuing the day's business. Faces and dress reveal a diverse racial mix of Jews, Romans, Greeks, and Arabs. Why should Sepphoris not have a cosmopolitan citizenry? Antipas' father was an Idumean, his mother a Samaritan, and his first wife the daughter of the Arab king, Aretas. The capital quite naturally attracts many with the promise of wealth and power—bureaucrats, scribes, priests, politicians, military officials, court favorites, scholars, merchants, architects, engineers, and artisans.

The main east-west street, lined with shops selling all manner of goods, leads to an inner wall where a second

Spring south of Sepphoris.

gate grants access to the acropolis and a scene of animated construction. Some beautiful public buildings stand completed; others are still being constructed. Architects and city planners have laid out the space on a grid plan, making the necessary adjustments to allow for the contours of the hill. Taunt strings outline the foundation trenches for the next building, a basilica to house the royal bank and government offices. Slaves, bodies glistening with sweat, dig the ditches for the footing and level the interior floor area. Architects closely supervise the work, for they know that these massive structures must be founded on the bedrock if they are to withstand the tests of weather and time. Heavy carts, drawn by four oxen, haul the white limestone ashlars from the nearby quarry up the inclined switchback road to the acropolis.

Large, oak-beam cranes lift the stones from the carts to the rising wall. The cranes, rigged with multiple pulleys, provide a mechanical advantage sufficient to handle the massive stones.[9] A master mason directs the placement of a large ashlar. "Bring it this way. Easy does it! Give me more slack. Careful now; hold it steady. Shore up that corner a little. Now ease it down. That's good!"

It is a thrilling sight, the thousands of workers—common laborers, skilled artisans, Roman construction soldiers[10]— swarming over the acropolis. Sepphoris rises like a shining Camelot. Woodsmen fell the tallest and straightest trees on the densely forested slopes close to the building site. They saw the logs to specified lengths and hew them into square beams, used for rafters to support the heavy red tile roof. Large saws slice some logs into planks that are then smoothed with long hand planes.

Carpenters busy themselves in a variety of essential jobs. Some erect scaffolding for the stone masons on the wall and also surround the tall slender Corinthian columns with additional scaffolding on which the mason sculpts the capital's delicate design of acanthus leaves. Carpenters fabricate the building's large oak doors and square the frames for the doors and windows. Finish carpenters skillfully build interior wood cabinets and furnishings. With simple hand tools a master carpenter produces beautiful results.

One team of carpenters assembles the sturdy semicircular forms that support the arches and extended vaults basic to Roman architecture.[11] Precisely cut stones are laid over these forms until keystones at the top are fitted snugly into place, locking the entire arch together. Then the wooden forms are removed and reused.

Some carpenters construct large cranes with ropes and pulleys that can lift the heavy stones and rafters. Other sure-footed carpenters walk the beams overhead and swing nimbly from rafter to rafter as they fit them solidly together.

Carpenters with special expertise lay out, cut, and assemble the parts of a waterwheel that can raise the water to the top of the acropolis. The wheel, approximately twelve feet in diameter, stands upright and rotates on its horizontal axis. A slave treading on the outer rim turns it. As the wheel rotates, wooden boxes around the outer rim dip into a lower pool and fill with water. The wheel then raises the water and pours it into a trough above. A series of these wheels can lift the water as high as necessary.[12]

It is an exciting scene, the coming to life of this brilliant new city. The forum in the center of the acropolis is surrounded by white limestone Roman-style buildings— here the theater, there the royal bank and archives, down that way Antipas' royal residence and the basilica for administrative offices, over here the Roman baths, and just there the Roman temple built in honor of the emperor Augustus.

Amid this flurry of activity, new and challenging cultural forces are at work in the heart of Galilee, forces that define the political, economic, and religious issues of Jesus' time. Jesus' ministry addresses people whose lives are swept up in the cross-cultural currents between the Jewish heritage and Antipas' puppet Roman government. The widespread response to Jesus' message from the people of the land, as well as the establishment, demonstrates that his teachings are both relevant and provocative.

The Gospels portray Jesus as a man who is acquainted with aspects of urban society and draws on images from city life to express his central message of the coming kingdom of God. These urban figures require a new appreciation of the man and his message incorporating the new information from Sepphoris.

An intriguing question arises from this investigation: "Did Jesus ever attend the theater?"

3

Jesus and
the Theater

"And when you pray, you must not be like the
hypocrites; for they love to stand and pray in
the synagogues and at the street corners, that
they may be seen by men. Truly, I say to you,
they have their reward. But when you pray, go
into your room and shut the door and pray to
your Father who is in secret; and your Father
who sees in secret will reward you."
(Matt. 6:5–6)

The above quotation and other Gospel passages raise the question, "Was Jesus
acquainted with stage actors?" The classical
Greek word _hypocritēs_, translated into
English as "hypocrite," primarily means
"stage actor," that is, one who plays a part
or pretends. The Greek word, _hypocritēs_, also describes a
person who practices deceit.[1] Occurring seventeen times in

Artist's reconstruction of the theater at Sepphoris.

the New Testament, *hypocritēs* is found only in the sayings of Jesus contained in the Synoptic Gospels (Matthew, Mark, and Luke). Jesus uses the image of an actor to criticize those whose religion is an external form rather than an inner fidelity to God. "The word [*hypocritēs*], derived from the theatre, denoted an actor, then one who played a part or acted a false role in public life; here [Matthew 6:2] used of people who want to be known as pious and so help the needy not in a generous sympathy but in a selfish effort to win praise from men."[2]

Jesus challenges his disciples to acknowledge the God who looks on the secret heart and to avoid a religious life of pretense and sham. "Such people are 'hypocrites' (literally, 'stage actors'). Out of a good deed which should be done in private they create a public spectacle, with themselves as director, producer, and star, bowing to the audience's applause. Hypocrisy is the split in a religious person between outward show and inner reality."[3]

In the Sermon on the Mount a recurring image is that of the "hypocrite" or "stage actor." The sermon appears to be a distillation of major themes in Jesus' teaching presented on various occasions (cf. Luke 6:17–38). The traditional setting is on the Mount of Beatitudes, a hill overlooking the northwest shore of the Sea of Galilee. The crowd follows Jesus to a quiet and restful setting, where they look down on the green slopes running to meet the lake's clear blue waters. Here and there sailboats dot the surface. Towns lining the shore bustle with people busy with the day's work. Across the lake to the east rises the high plateau of the Golan, beyond which flourish the Greek cities of the Decapolis. Through the haze a sharp eye can make out the point on the lake's south end where the Jordan River begins its serpentine descent toward the Dead Sea.

In this pastoral setting Jesus draws on urban images that reflect a shared awareness of the actor's art and calls his disciples to a genuine commitment to God's

Bedouin shepherd boy near the traditional site of the Sermon on the Mount.

sovereignty over all of life. "And when you pray," he says, "you must not be like the hypocrites; for they love to stand and pray in the synagogues and at the street corners, that they may be seen by men" (Matt. 6:5).[4] This public display of piety is a performance calculated to impress the observers. Like actors repeating their lines on stage with studied gestures and inflections, these religious figures recite their prayers just to be seen.

When their performance is finished and their audience sufficiently impressed, they have achieved their purpose and have their reward. But, Jesus' disciples should pray behind closed doors in the privacy of their rooms. In solitude, before the Father who understands the secrets of life, the disciple attunes the human spirit to the Divine. This God met in the inner seclusion of room and heart will richly reward those opening their lives to his will in honest prayer. Jesus' own life exemplifies the power of prayer both in the crises and in the routine of his ministry.

Jesus admonishes his followers to refrain from empty phrases or mindless repetitions. Their prayers may be modeled on this prayer:

> Our Father who art in heaven,
> Hallowed be thy name.
> Thy kingdom come,
> Thy will be done,
>   On earth as it is in heaven.
> Give us this day our daily bread;
> And forgive us our debts,
>   As we also have forgiven our debtors;
> And lead us not into temptation,
>   But deliver us from evil. (Matt. 6:9–13)

When Jesus' disciples bestow alms or make charitable donations, they must not seek honor and public acclaim by, figuratively speaking, sounding a trumpet in the synagogue or streets—like an actor whose dramatic entrance on stage is announced with a trumpet's fanfare. "To sound the trumpet, a metaphorical expression comparable to 'toot your own horn,' is likely drawn from the fact that rams' horns were blown and alms were given at the autumn public fasts for rain."[5] Eleemosynary gifts should be privately made so that the left hand does not know "what [the] right hand is doing . . . and your Father who sees in secret will reward you" (Matt. 6:3–4).

Once when Jesus sat opposite the temple treasury watching people putting in their money, he observed many rich people making charitable donations. Then a poor widow put in two small copper coins. Jesus said that this woman had contributed more than all the rest. "For they all contributed out of their abundance; but she out of her poverty has put in everything she had, her whole living" (Mark 12:41–44; cf. Luke 21:1–4). Kahlil Gibran expressed this idea with these words: "Is not dread of thirst when your well is full, the thirst that is unquenchable? There are those who give little of the much which they have—and they give it for recognition and their hidden desire makes their gifts unwholesome. And there are those who have little and give it all. These are the believers in life and the bounty of life, and their coffer is never empty. There are those who give with joy, and that joy is their reward."[6]

"When you fast," Jesus instructs his hearers, "do not look dismal, like the hypocrites, for they disfigure their faces that their fasting may be seen by men" (Matt. 6:16). It was customary during a religious fast, as an expression of grief or sorrow for sins, to dress in sack cloth, tear one's clothes, and place ashes on the head. This appearance, accompanied by a long and somber face, was an open display of fasting. The comparison appears to be with the tragic actor who makes up his face to portray dramatically the agony of his character. In the theaters of the Roman provinces, actors or mimes frequently preferred makeup instead of dramatic masks, because it allowed greater flexibility of facial expressions in the portrayal of the character.[7] Subtle nuances could be communicated by the distortion of the mouth or a side glance.

If Jesus' disciples fast (see Mark 2:19), their contrite spirits are lifted up to their merciful Father. With the assurance of God's forgiveness, they can wash their faces and anoint their heads, facing the world confidently in the conviction that God sees and forgives.

The image of a comic actor in a farce is conjured by Jesus' warning about criticizing others (Matt. 7:1–5). "Judge not, that you be not judged," he says. You will receive the same judgment that you give. He instructs his disciples not to be like an actor who attempts to remove a speck from his brother's eye while he has a log lodged in his own eye. One cannot but smile at the ludicrous scene brought to mind by this gross exaggeration.

Jesus' Exposure to Theaters

Where could Jesus have become acquainted with actors and the theater?

We will address this obvious question before exploring the other instances in which Jesus speaks of actors. The closest theater, only four miles from Jesus' home in Nazareth, was at Sepphoris. Archaeological excavations directed by Leroy Waterman in 1931 discovered this theater and dated its construction to the time of Antipas (or perhaps earlier, to the reign of his father, Herod the Great).[8] Subsequent excavations in the 1980s directed by James F. Strange confirmed the Antipas date.[9] This means that the theater was constructed while Jesus was a young man in Nazareth. A person visiting the capital would be impressed by this imposing white limestone structure built into the north face of the acropolis.

The beautiful theater at Sepphoris was the newest and the nearest to Nazareth. There were several other

Girl cleaning carved stone.

theaters in the areas where Jesus traveled. Almost a decade before Antipas was born, his father, Herod the Great, built the lavish theater at Jerusalem as part of his preparation to celebrate the Actium Games in 28 B.C. This celebration honored Octavian's victory over Antony and Cleopatra. According to Luke (2:41–42), when Jesus was twelve he accompanied his parents on their annual pilgrimage to Jerusalem at passover. On these trips, it is probable that Jesus became acquainted with this theater.

Herod the Great acquired the reputation as a theater builder. He erected a theater at his winter palace in Jericho and another in the fortified City of Samaria (which he renamed Sebaste, the Greek translation of Augustus). The Gospels say that during his brief public ministry Jesus traveled in the vicinity of both Jericho and Samaria (Mark 10:46; John 4:3–6); these cities were on the two main pilgrim routes between Galilee and Jerusalem. Herod built a theater in his port city of Caesarea Maritima, and even constructed a theater in Sidon just north of his kingdom as a sign of friendship toward these neighboring peoples. Jesus also traveled in the district of Tyre and Sidon (Phoenicia—Matt. 15:21; Mark 7:24, 31).

Mark notes that Jesus went through the region of the Decapolis east of the Sea of Galilee (Mark 7:31; cf. 5:20). Matthew adds that people from the Decapolis comprised a significant part of the crowds that followed Jesus and heard the Sermon on the Mount (Matt. 4:25). The people in these ten Greek cities primarily spoke Greek. Theaters were a standard feature of their city architecture and exerted a strong and pervasive influence on their culture. While there were a number of theaters in the areas where Jesus traveled, the theater at Sepphoris provided the closest setting in which the youthful Jesus could become acquainted with actors.

Cameo of Augustus.

The Theater at Sepphoris

Antipas' theater at Sepphoris was a natural expression of the values he had received through his education in Rome during the Augustan Golden Age. Shortly before Antipas arrived in Rome in 8 B.C., Augustus had dedicated the Theater of Marcellus, the third permanent theater to be erected in the Imperial City. Augustus was an avid patron of education and the performing arts and frequently attended theatrical performances. In fact, during Augustus' reign, forty days each year were devoted to theater plays performed in connection with religious festivals.[10] It was during this heyday of Roman drama that Antipas must have developed his appreciation for the stage and its cultural and political importance.

Augustus' love of the theater is seen in the account of his death. Aware that the icy hand of death gripped him, he called for a mirror and had his personal servant comb his hair and lift his sagging jaw. Then he summoned his closest friends who gathered silently about the dying emperor's bed. He inquired of them if he had played well his part in life's brief comedy. "Yes!" they answered reassuringly. Then Augustus, with a fading twinkle in his closing eyes, said, "Since well I've played my part, all clap your hands and from the stage dismiss me with applause."[11] They gave him a standing ovation.

When Antipas built his four-thousand-seat theater at Sepphoris, his architects followed the basic plan of the Theater of Marcellus in Rome. Marcus Vitruvius Pollio, the architect appointed by Augustus to manage the elaborate and all important waterworks for the City of Rome, wrote a treatise on architecture in which he laid out the blueprint for constructing a theater. Since the theater at Sepphoris was the closest to Jesus' home in Nazareth, it merits special attention.

In the summer of 1986, after the rubble had been cleared from the theater, James F. Strange gave a lecture there to about forty volunteers. They sat around on the steps chiseled into the bedrock that had once supported the smoothly polished white limestone seats. Virtually all these fine stone seats had been robbed out and reused in later buildings, but the few remaining gave testimony to the once splendid seating. I moved to different locations in the theater and was impressed that even now the acoustics are remarkably good.

As I sat watching and listening to Jim's lecture, I imagined how the theater must have looked in Jesus' day when it was new and bright in the summer's sun. In my mind I rebuilt the theater on its existing foundations. The surviving stone seats *in situ,* the column drums, their bases and Corinthian capitals, and the highly decorated

James F. Strange lecturing in the theater at Sepphoris.

stone fragments all came together, like the dry bones in the prophet Ezekiel's vision of the valley of death.

I was helped in this reconstruction by Vitruvius' description of how to lay out a theater as well as comparisons with other Roman theaters from this period. The design of a theater begins by drawing a circle whose radius is equal to that of the orchestra. The circumference of this circle is then divided into twelve equal segments, like the signs of the zodiac.[12] It is easier to think of this circle as the face of a clock. A line drawn through nine and three o'clock bisects the circle and determines the line separating the orchestra from the front of the stage. A parallel line drawn through ten and two o'clock locates the back of the stage or the front of the stage building, the *scaenae frons.* The numbers three through nine located on the arc circumscribing the orchestra fix the points where the stairs radiate up into the seats of the *cavea.*

The stage of the theater at Sepphoris was large, measuring 156 feet wide and 27 feet from front to back. The wooden floor helped to resonate the actors' voices. The stage building was more than two stories high. Its facade was beautifully decorated with slender columns and pilasters, and intricately carved stone work. The overhanging roof sloped upward to reflect sound to the audience in the last row. In the stage building were three imposing entrances. The center door, the largest, was the king's door (*aula regia*), designed as the entrance to a royal palace. This door was flanked on either side by two guest doors (*hospitalia*). Two additional exits were located at the side wings (*itinera versurarum*).[13]

The smooth white limestone seats of the *cavea* rose up sharply to meet the semicircular colonnade behind the top row. Not only aesthetically pleasing, this covered colonnade provided the audience shelter in the event of a sudden shower.[14]

The production of a classical drama usually required sets to assist the audience in imagining the setting for the

Column base in baulk.

actors on stage. Vitruvius describes how these tall three-sided sets were constructed. Their bases were in the shape of equilateral triangles; each of the three sides was painted with a different scene.[15] One side depicted a royal setting like a palace. A second side was painted to resemble a landscape with trees, mountains, and caves. The third portrayed a domestic scene with private homes that had doors, windows, and balconies. When a change of scenery was required, these sets, or "machines" as Vitruvius calls them, were rotated one-third turn.

A large curtain (*aulaeum*) painted with elaborate scenery could be raised and lowered with ropes and pulleys into a trench between the stage and the scene building. Additionally, smaller pleated curtains (*siparia*), attached to the scene building, could be either lowered or drawn to the side to change the scenery.[16]

The Romans learned a great deal about the science of acoustics from the Greeks, who had carefully calculated how to create the best sound quality in the theater. Vitruvius describes one significant technological development involving the use of large bronze resonance vases throughout the theater. These vases were positioned in designated rows and were of varying sizes depending on the distance to the stage. The vases were placed upside down on wedges in stone boxes. The boxes had open tops and an open slot at the floor level on the side facing the stage. Sound entering through the slot resonated in the vase and was amplified. Vitruvius maintains that this technique was widely used in theaters where Greek influence had spread, although he points out that in some theaters earthenware vases were substituted for bronze.[17] Since the stones of the theater at Sepphoris have been robbed out, there is no hard evidence that the theater had such a sound system. But it is likely that Antipas would have used the best technology to make Sepphoris the jewel of Galilee.

The use to which Antipas put his theater is not described in extant documents. The design, quality of construction, size, and location (at the top of the acropolis) clearly indicates the central place that it served in the cultural life of the capital. Some light may be cast on the functions of the theater by comparison with contemporary theaters of which Antipas could have had knowledge.

Herod the Great had constructed his lavish theater at Jerusalem before Antipas was born in order to celebrate the Actium Games. These games, inaugurated in 28 B.C. in honor of Octavian's victory over Antony and Cleopatra, were celebrated every four (or perhaps five) years. Josephus writes that the theater was the setting for elaborate musical and dramatic competitions attended by celebrities from throughout Herod's kingdom and beyond. To encourage excellence in these performing arts Herod awarded high honors and generous prizes to the winners.[18] There was a long-standing tradition in the Eastern monarchies for the king to sponsor theatrical guilds for dramatic and musical crafts associated with the god Dionysus.[19]

Antipas studied in Rome during a period when Augustus avidly sponsored the theater. Classical dramas by famous Greek playwrights—Menander, Apollodorus, Philemon, Demophilus—had been adapted by Plautus, Terence, and others for the Roman stage.[20] These productions may well have defined for Antipas and his advisors the dramas that were currently fashionable.

An interesting and significant fragment of a tragic drama written in Greek by a second-century B.C. Jewish playwright, Ezekiel the Tragedian, is from *The Exagoge* or *The Exodus.* Ezekiel's drama, an adaptation of the biblical story for the stage, demonstrates that some Jews considered the theater an appropriate setting for teaching both the Jewish youth and Gentiles of God's mighty acts in the Jews' history. It is significant that the voice of God is heard from the stage speaking to Moses from the burning bush.

But, unlike the Greek and Roman dramatic productions, in which an actor dressed as a god was lowered onto the stage with a crane (*deus ex machina*), the Hebrews' God remains unseen. In one very poignant passage the voice of God is heard saying to Moses, "Take courage, O child, and listen to my words. For you cannot see my face since you are mortal, but my words you are allowed to hear."[21]

The theater also provided an appropriate setting for poetry readings, lectures, orations, public policy addresses, and meetings of the city council (*boulē*). Josephus tells of an appearance in A.D. 44 made by Agrippa I in the theater at Caesarea, less than thirty miles from Sepphoris.[22] Agrippa celebrated a festival in honor of the emperor and invited a large number of government officials and men of high rank. When they had assembled in the theater at dawn, Agrippa appeared on stage dressed in a wonderful robe woven of silver. The robe shimmered in the first rays of the sun while Agrippa delivered his oration seated on a throne (Acts 12:20–23). The audience called out that Agrippa was more than mortal, indeed a god. Agrippa basked in their flattery, until looking up he saw an owl perched on a rope overhead. He took this to be an evil omen and immediately became seriously ill, experiencing sharp pains in his chest and stomach. He died five days later.

The Theater in the Teachings of Jesus

The presence of several theaters in the areas where Jesus traveled offered opportunities for him and his audience to become acquainted with actors and the stage. The recurring image of the actor in Jesus' teachings suggests a person who pretends or plays a role. The actor provides a vivid comparison with the religious showman whose affected piety has become a public performance. Jesus primarily censures the religious establishment who substitute outward form for inner faith. But, the criticism applies to all whose religious lives are devoid of genuine commitment to God's sovereignty or "the kingdom of heaven."

The actor or hypocrite is a favorite image in Matthew and reflects a period when there were mounting tensions between church and synagogue. This conflict, however, began during the ministry of Jesus. Matthew repeats the invective, "Woe to you, scribes and Pharisees, hypocrites!" to introduce Jesus' critiques. By their traditions these religious actors shut people out of the kingdom of heaven and yet refuse to enter themselves (Matt. 23:13). With great missionary zeal, they search land and sea to win a convert and then make the poor proselyte doubly a "child of hell" or a slave to their religious forms.

Jesus points out that these actors carefully tithe trivial spices—mint, dill, and cummin—but disregard the important values of the law for society—justice, mercy, faith. "You blind guides, straining out a gnat and swallowing a camel!" (Matt. 23:24). These thespians' preoccupation with appearances to the neglect of genuine purity of heart is aptly compared by Jesus to washing a cup outside while leaving the inside filthy with extortion and greed. Drink and become ill! The comparison is drawn even more graphically by depicting these hypocrites as whitewashed tombs. They beautify the exterior and paint the outside but are filled with death and decay. "So you also outwardly appear righteous to men, but within you are full of hypocrisy and iniquity" (Matt. 23:28). While the pretentious religious leaders may erect tombs for the prophets and decorate monuments in honor of the righteous, they are reluctant to assume a prophetic stance in an unjust society. It is easier to profess social justice than to be just (Matt. 23:29–36). Jesus' complaint is not against actors but against pretense and sham.

Luke tells the story of Jesus healing a woman on the sabbath in a synagogue. For eighteen years she had suffered from a curvature of the spine that made it impossible for her to stand straight. Jesus saw her and said,

"Woman, you are freed from your infirmity." Then he laid his hands on her and she stood upright. The woman praised God but the ruler of the synagogue rebuked Jesus. "There are six days on which work ought to be done; come on those days and be healed, and not on the sabbath day." Jesus noted that hypocrites or actors would untie an ox or an ass on the sabbath and lead it to water. Should not this woman also on the sabbath day be loosed from her infirmity? (Luke 13:10–17).

The disparity between the observance of outward traditions and a sincere commitment to the will of God, expressed through the image of the actor, is spotlighted by the story concerning the washing of hands before eating. Some Pharisees and scribes from Jerusalem interrogated Jesus: "Why do your disciples not live according to the tradition of the elders, but eat with hands defiled?" Jesus replied that actors play the very role prophesied by Isaiah, who said, "This people honors me with their lips, but their heart is far from me; in vain do they worship me, teaching as doctrines the precepts of men" (Mark 7:1–8; cf. Isa. 29:13).

One afternoon as the shadows grew long and Sepphoris fell silent I strolled to the great theater and sat down with my thoughts. Imagination peoples the stage with a touring drama company rehearsing a scene from the *Trojan Women,* the famous tragedy written by Euripides to protest Athenian imperialism, after its destruction of the Island of Melos. Pots billow forth black smoke against the painted sets of a destroyed city. Word on the street is that Antipas has selected this tragedy to remind the citizens of Sepphoris of the city's destruction by Varus in 4 B.C. and to warn them of the folly of revolt against Rome.

Hecuba, yesterday queen of Troy, today a helpless widow consigned to slavery, laments her city's fate: "Troy is in smoke, let us weep for Troy. Like a mother hen clucking over her fluttering chicks, I shall lead your song [of sorrow]." I recall the lament of Jesus from the Mount of

Olives as he looks across at Jerusalem and envisions the coming destruction. "O Jerusalem, Jerusalem, killing the prophets and stoning those who are sent to you! How often would I have gathered your children together as a hen gathers her brood under her wings, and you would not! Behold your house is forsaken and desolate" (Matt. 23:37–38; cf. Luke 13:34–35). Is it possible, I wonder, that the measured style and dramatic quality of his parables, that so brilliantly discover meanings in commonplace scenes, could have drawn on the dramatic and visual power of the stage? Could it be, I muse, that watching a tragic hero pursue his fate to his inevitable destiny prompted Jesus to set his face toward Jerusalem as the only appropriate arena in which to challenge the establishment and to be executed?

Continuing excavations at Sepphoris have raised the curtain on a new act in the ongoing drama of Jesus and the movement that cast him in the leading role. The stage on which he acted out his ministry was cosmopolitan and sophisticated and his understanding of urban life more relevant than previously imagined.

4

Antipas the Fox and John the Baptist

[Jesus] began to speak to the crowds concerning John: "What did you go out into the wilderness to behold? A reed shaken by the wind? What then did you go out to see? A man clothed in soft raiment? Behold, those who are gorgeously appareled and live in luxury are in kings' courts." (Luke 7:24–25)

When Antipas built Sepphoris and Tiberias, he constructed opulent palaces and enjoyed the pleasures of an oriental monarch. Jesus contrasts the austere life-style of John the Baptist in the Jordan wilderness with the luxury of the king's court. The shadow of Antipas the tetrarch, or king as he is often referred to in the Gospels, falls across several of their pages. Antipas beheaded John the Baptist and attempted unsuccessfully to arrest and execute Jesus. Warned by some Pharisees that Antipas wanted to kill him, Jesus responded, "Go and tell that fox, 'Behold, I cast out demons and perform cures today and tomorrow, and the third day I finish my course'" (Luke 13:32). During Jesus' trial in Jerusalem, Pilate sent him to Antipas to be interrogated but Antipas returned Jesus without finding him guilty of any crime (Luke 23:6–12). How did Antipas influence the careers of John and Jesus?

John the Baptist, according to the Gospel of Luke, preached in the region near the Jordan River during the fifteenth year of the emperor Tiberius' reign, about A.D. 29 (Luke 3:1).[1] Luke understands John's ministry as the fulfillment of Isaiah's prophecy, "The voice of one crying in the wilderness: Prepare the way of the Lord, make his paths straight. . . . and all flesh shall see the salvation of God" (Luke 3:4, 6; cf. Isa. 40:3, 5). This prophecy also was used by the Essenes at Qumran, who produced the Dead Sea Scrolls, to describe their mission in the wilderness.

John was a striking preacher with a strong message. Clothed in a camel's hair garment cinched at the waist with a wide leather girdle, John cut a curious figure. He refused to eat bread or drink wine (Luke 7:33) but instead ate locusts and wild honey (Mark 1:6). It was not his hermit like appearance but his message that attracted large crowds from the region of the Jordan and from Judea and Jerusalem. John preached a baptism of repentance for forgiveness of sins and announced that "the kingdom of heaven is at hand" (Mark 1:4; Luke 3:3; Matt. 3:2). To usher in this kingdom, one more powerful than John would soon arrive. "I baptize you with water," John declared, "but he who is mightier than I is coming, the thong of whose sandals I am not worthy to untie; he will baptize you with the Holy Spirit and with fire" (Luke 3:16).

Antipas with his architects.

Headwaters of the
Jordan River.

In view of the seriousness of sin and the nearness of the kingdom, John harangued his audience, "You brood of vipers! Who warned you to flee from the wrath to come?" Being the descendants of Abraham offered false security from the impending judgment. "Even now the axe is laid to the root of the trees; every tree therefore that does not bear good fruit is cut down and thrown into the fire" (Luke 3:7–9). John's bold message carried the challenge to reject sin and to do the will of God.

From the audience came questions about specific responsibilities implied by John's grand proclamation. He responded that the sharing of possessions must characterize the life of repentance. Food and clothing should be distributed to those in genuine need. Tax collectors must be honest, collecting "no more than is appointed you." Soldiers should be satisfied with their pay and not use violence and intimidation to extort money from the defenseless (Luke 3:10–14).

John stressed that the harvest indeed had come! The "mightier one" would arrive at the threshing floor of judgment. Winnowing fork in hand, he would separate the wheat from the chaff. The wheat would be stored in the granary and the chaff consumed with fire. Soon Jesus came from Galilee, heard John preach, approved of his ministry, and accepted his baptism. The casual observer would have thought of Jesus as another disciple of the Baptist. Matthew underscores John's reluctance to baptize Jesus, whom John recognized to be his superior (Matt. 3:13–15). Following the baptism, the Holy Spirit descended on Jesus in the form of a dove and a voice from heaven announced, "This is my beloved Son, with whom I am well pleased" (Matt. 3:17).

John directed his demand for repentance toward Antipas, who recently had divorced his first wife and married his sister-in-law, Herodias.[2] John condemned the marriage publicly because marrying a living brother's wife was contrary to the Mosaic law.[3] Antipas responded by having John arrested and imprisoned.[4]

Who was Antipas' first wife? Soon after the youthful Antipas began the construction of his new capital at Sepphoris in 3 B.C., he married a proud Arabian princess, the daughter of Aretas IV, king of Nabataea.[5] Aretas had sent his troops to assist Varus, the governor of Syria, to crush the rebellions that broke out following Herod the Great's death. Sepphoris was a major town plundered and burned by Aretas' forces during this campaign. It was to his new royal residence at Sepphoris that Antipas brought his Nabataean bride.

Antipas' marriage had clear political and economic advantages. Nabataea encompassed Palestine on the south and east, and shared some forty miles of border with Antipas' Peraea. The Nabataeans controlled the lucrative caravan trade routes in this vast territory and became a proud, powerful, and prosperous people.[6] Aretas ruled from his capital at Petra, often called "the rose red city, half as old as time." The marvelous ruins of this ancient city are preserved today, carved into the multicolored sandstone in a hidden valley forty-five miles south of the Dead Sea. Antipas' marriage ratified a strong and valuable alliance with his fierce neighbors, granting important trade concessions and promising mutual nonaggression. The long period of peaceful relations that Antipas enjoyed with Aretas suggests that the marriage had a considerable degree of success.

About A.D. 29 Antipas made a trip to Rome to settle some affairs of state at the imperial court of Tiberius. On the way he visited a half brother who probably lived in Caesarea.[7] During this stay, Antipas became enamored of Herodias, his brother's wife, and secretly proposed marriage. Herodias accepted the offer and pledged to marry Antipas when he had returned from Rome, provided that he would get rid of his Arab wife. Antipas agreed and sailed to Rome.[8]

His business in Rome complete, Antipas returned to Galilee. But the word of his secret arrangement with Herodias somehow had reached his wife. She pretended to be unaware of Antipas' intended marriage to Herodias and asked innocently to visit their lavish fortress palace at Machaerus that guarded the border between Peraea and her homeland of Nabataea. Antipas gladly granted her request, knowing that it was an opportune time for her to be away. No sooner had she reached Machaerus than she escaped over the border with prearranged help from trusted friends. She hastened to Petra and recounted to her father, King Aretas, the planned marriage between Antipas and Herodias. Aretas understood that this second marriage and the rejection of his daughter had broken both the familial and political bonds with Antipas and patiently sought an opportunity to settle the score.[9]

Petra.

With his Nabataean wife out of the picture, Antipas
married Herodias who recently had divorced her husband. She moved with her young daughter, Salome, to
the royal palace at Tiberias that overlooked the Sea of
Galilee. Shortly after, John began his public verbal
assault on King Antipas "for all the evil things that
Herod had done" (Luke 3:19), especially for his marriage
to his living brother's wife. The marriage was a clear violation of the ancient Mosaic law (Lev. 18:16; 20:21).

Herodias was incensed at John's vehement rebukes and probably would have had John assassinated had not Antipas arrested, bound, and imprisoned John in the fortress of Machaerus.[10] Antipas did not wish to make a martyr of John, who had become a popular prophetic figure. But neither could Antipas stand idly by while John railed out against him. With the threat of Aretas looming on the horizon like the dark cloud of a desert dust storm, Antipas could ill afford an uprising within his own borders.[11] With John safe in prison his movement began to lose momentum.

The fortress of Machaerus, located five miles east of the Dead Sea near the border between Peraea and Nabataea, was situated atop a high mountain. Its natural rocky eminence surrounded by deep ravines made it virtually unassailable. Herod the Great, as he had done at Masada and Herodium, crowned the summit with a massive fortress palace protected by strong ramparts and tall corner towers. The garrison quartered in the fortress possessed a large supply of weapons and engines of war capable of repelling virtually any attack.[12]

Josephus says that at the foot of the mountain there were a number of natural springs, some flowing with hot water and others with cold. Near these springs Herod built a town with relaxing baths.[13]

Mark (6:20) relates that while John was imprisoned Antipas took the occasion to interrogate him. Although educated in Rome, Antipas respected John as a righteous and holy man and welcomed the opportunity to converse with him. Yet Antipas was deeply troubled and perplexed by what John had to say. One can easily envision John in his camel's hair garment and leather girdle standing bound before Antipas in his splendid purple robe and seated in an audience chamber within the fortress.

King Antipas obviously would ask John the purpose of his movement and the nature of his demand for repentance. John repeated his public proclamation. "I told your tax collectors to be honest and your soldiers to be content with their wages and not to extort with violence. I encouraged those who genuinely repented to share their food and clothing with those in need. And as you well know, I criticized your marriage to your brother's wife, because it is a blatant violation of God's demand set forth in the Law of Moses."

Antipas' informers developed a profile on John whose sharp criticisms of Antipas' policies—especially his adulterous marriage to Herodias—and widespread popularity could inflame a revolt.[14] When Antipas asked John about his messianic views, John responded, "I told those who inquired of me, that I am not the messiah or Christ but one, mightier than I, will soon come who will baptize his followers with the Holy Spirit and with fire" (see Luke 3:15–16). This claim disturbed Antipas, for it raised questions. When will the messiah come? Where will he be found? How will he be recognized? What reforms will he bring about? Will they be military, political, economic, religious? Has the messiah even now arrived on the scene? Will he disturb the fragile peace?

In prison John heard from his disciples about Jesus' ministry and was confronted again with the question of Jesus' true identity. John sent two of his disciples to ask Jesus, "Are you he who is to come, or shall we look for another?" (Matt. 11:3; Luke 7:19). Antipas, for his own reasons, was also keenly interested in Jesus' answer. Jesus, knowing that John was in the clutches of Antipas, the fox, cautiously equivocates: "Go and tell John what you hear and see: the blind receive their sight and the lame walk, lepers are cleansed and the deaf hear, and the dead are raised up, and the poor have good news preached to them. And blessed is he who takes no offense at me" (Matt. 11:4–6; cf. Luke 7:22–23). When John's messengers had departed, Jesus remarked to the crowds that John was no ordinary prophet. "I tell you," Jesus said, "among those born of women none is greater than John; yet he who is least in the kingdom of God is greater than he" (Luke 7:28).

Matters came to a head between John and Antipas when the latter celebrated his birthday—probably his fiftieth. In attendance were the leading men of Galilee as well as Antipas' courtiers and officers. The secretary of finance, Chuza, whose wife became a follower and supporter of Jesus, would have a prominent place at the feast. During the celebration while the guests were eating and drinking their fill, Salome, Herodias' teenage daughter, entertained them with a graceful and provocative dance. Antipas, flushed with enthusiasm at the lovely young girl's charming and exotic movements, rashly offered over his cup of wine to grant her any wish, even half of his kingdom. Salome respectfully excused herself from the banquet hall and consulted with Herodias concerning what she should ask from her stepfather. Without hesitation Herodias coldly replied, "John's head!" Salome returned to Antipas and before all the important guests stated her request, "I want you to give me at once the head of John the Baptist on a platter" (Matt. 14:8; Mark 6:25).

Antipas, somewhat sobered by the young girl's request, suddenly realized that he had played into Herodias' hands. But, he had made his oath—rash though it was—before the most influential and important men of his realm and could not renege. Reluctantly Antipas gave the order and a soldier of the guard went to the prison and there with a powerful blow cut off John's head. The severed head was served on a platter to Salome, who in turn presented it to her vengeful mother.

Without their martyred leader, John's disciples were thrown into disarray. Some continued to revere John's memory and remained loyal to his cause (see Acts 19:1–7). Others joined those who already had left John to follow Jesus (John 1:37). Reports of the accelerating growth of Jesus' movement soon reached Antipas, who feared that Jesus was John the Baptist returned from the

grave to haunt him (Matt. 14:2; Mark 6:14; Luke 9:7).
Antipas gave the order to arrest Jesus and bring him for
interrogation (Luke 9:9). Some Pharisees suspected that
once Antipas had Jesus in his grasp, Antipas would kill
him (Luke 13:31). Jesus turned aside their warning, saying, "Go and tell that fox . . . 'I must go on my way today
and tomorrow and the day following; for it cannot be
that a prophet should perish away from Jerusalem'"
(Luke 13:32–33). Jesus, however, took care to avoid being
arrested by Antipas' police.

Josephus adds an interesting footnote to his story of
Antipas the king and John the Baptist's death. After
Antipas divorced King Aretas' daughter in order to marry
Herodias, Aretas sought an opportunity for revenge. An
occasion to begin hostilities presented itself with a border
dispute in A.D. 36.[15] Aretas mustered his troops under his
able commander and Antipas sent his forces to counter the
advance. As the two armies prepared for battle, the plan of
attack of Antipas' general was leaked to Aretas' commander. In the ensuing engagement, Antipas' soldiers took
heavy casualties and were completely routed. Immediately
Antipas sent a report of Aretas' aggression to the emperor
Tiberius, who ordered the governor of Syria, Vitellius, to
move with full military strength against Aretas. The message concluded, "Send Aretas or his head to me!"[16]

Many Jews considered Antipas' humiliating defeat to
be divine punishment for killing John the Baptist, who
was thought to be a good man. His call to repentance
and his challenge to lead lives dedicated to righteousness
and justice were godly summons sealed in baptism.[17]

The final tragic episode in Antipas' long and relatively
stable rule over Galilee and Peraea again involved Herodias. Her brother, Agrippa, returned in A.D. 38 to Palestine
from Rome with the title of king over the territory northeast of the Sea of Galilee.[18] Agrippa had been a prodigal
son, wasting his inheritance in a carefree, playboy life-
style. Reduced to poverty, he soon acquired large debts

that he had no way of repaying. Antipas attempted to help his brother-in-law and appointed him to the civil service post of market inspector for the new capital, Tiberias. But Antipas lost no opportunity to remind Agrippa, and others, that he was an irresponsible spendthrift and financially dependent on Antipas' good will.[19]

Hounded by his creditors, Agrippa paid off old debts with new loans. Finally, dissatisfied with his lackluster life in Tiberias, he borrowed enough money to sail to Rome, where he became a close friend of Gaius, the nephew of the emperor Tiberius. One day Agrippa, in an unguarded moment, said aloud to Gaius that it would be fortunate if Tiberius would relinquish his throne to Gaius, who was much more competent to rule. Word of this reached Tiberius and Agrippa was imprisoned in chains.[20] As fate would have it, Tiberius died six months later after conferring the empire upon Gaius. Soon Emperor Gaius Caligula freed his good friend, Agrippa, and gave him a chain of gold equal in weight to the one with which Tiberius had bound him. In addition, Gaius made Agrippa king of the territory northeast of the Sea of Galilee.[21]

When Agrippa returned to Palestine to secure his kingdom, Herodias could not bear the thought of her spendthrift brother becoming a king while her husband, after more than forty years of successful rule, remained officially only a tetrarch. She prevailed upon Antipas to sail to Rome and obtain the title of king to which he was certainly entitled. Antipas, content with the status quo, at first was reluctant to become embroiled in the power politics of Gaius Caligula's imperial court. Herodias would not take "no" for an answer and egged Antipas on until he finally agreed. After elaborate and expensive preparations, they set sail.[22]

Agrippa, apprised of the purpose of their voyage, wrote a letter to Gaius charging Antipas with treason. Agrippa informed the emperor that Antipas had manufactured

Gold chain from Sepphoris.

and stockpiled weapons and armor sufficient to equip fully an army of 70,000. Antipas, Agrippa wrote, planned to join forces with the Parthians in a revolt against Rome.

When Antipas and Herodias appeared before Gaius, he was reading Agrippa's letter. Gaius asked Antipas if he possessed the military equipment that Agrippa accused him of having. Antipas could not deny that he had the armor and weapons, although he insisted that they were only for defensive purposes. Gaius took this admission as sufficient evidence to exile Antipas on the spot to southern France and to add his lands and possessions to Agrippa's kingdom.

Gaius learned that Herodias was Agrippa's sister and offered to treat her as the sister of a loyal client king of Rome rather than the wife of a deposed tetrarch. To his generous proposal Herodias proudly responded that she had enjoyed the good years with Antipas and now she would accept the bad. Although angered by her refusal, Gaius granted her wish and sent her to share Antipas' exile.[23]

Antipas was almost sixty years old when he was exiled in A.D. 39. For forty-two years he had ruled successfully as tetrarch over Galilee and Peraea—first from his new capital, Sepphoris, and later from Tiberias. But, Herodias aroused his ambition to be designated king. Overweening pride stripped him of power, possessions, and prestige. Antipas became a truly tragic figure as he and Herodias were sent into exile, where they faded from the pages of history—outfoxed by Agrippa.

5

The King Figure in the Teachings of Jesus

> *Then turning to the disciples he said privately,*
> *"Blessed are the eyes which see what you see!*
> *For I tell you that many prophets and kings*
> *desired to see what you see, and did not see it,*
> *and to hear what you hear, and did not hear*
> *it." (Luke 10:23–24)*

Jesus lived most of his life four miles from the capital, Sepphoris, where Antipas built his royal residence and ruled as a Roman client king, or tetrarch. The image of king occurs in a number of parables and sayings attributed to Jesus in the Gospels. How do these sayings represent the figure of the king? What are his most obvious characteristics? Is the king's use of power corrupt or enlightened? Was Jesus' understanding of kingship influenced by a knowledge of Antipas' policies and rule? Does the image of the king reveal significant insights into Jesus' central message of the coming kingdom of God? How does Jesus view life at the royal court?

From prison John the Baptist sends two of his disciples to ask Jesus if he is the one anticipated by John's ministry or if they should look for someone else. Jesus tells them to report to John the healings that he has performed. After they depart, Jesus asks the crowds what they had gone to see in the wilderness: "A man clothed in soft raiment?" Then Jesus alludes to the ease and luxury characteristic of Antipas' life-style. "Behold, those who wear soft raiment are in kings' houses" (Matt. 11:8). Or as Luke phrases it, "Behold, those who are gorgeously appareled and live in luxury are in kings' courts" (Luke 7:25).

The Herodian family constructed a number of opulent palaces at strategic locations. Herod the Great built palaces in Jerusalem and Jericho, as well as in the fortresses at Masada, Herodium, and Machaerus. Antipas also erected royal palaces at both Sepphoris and Tiberias. The luxury and ostentation of the Herodian court were legendary and no expense was spared to keep alive its conspicuous affluence.

One of Jesus' followers was Joanna, the wife of Antipas' finance minister, Chuza. She followed Jesus about Galilee along with several other women, who together underwrote the expenses of his itinerant ministry (Luke 8:3). Joanna could easily have informed Jesus of the splendid style in which Antipas and his court officials lived. The excesses and extravagances of the royal family stood in sharp contrast to the conditions of the poor peasants dwelling on the land. Jesus alludes to his own homelessness: "Foxes have holes, and birds of the air have nests; but the Son of man has nowhere to lay his head" (Matt. 8:20; Luke 9:58).

The Parable of the Unjust Steward

Once Peter asks Jesus, "Lord, how often shall my brother sin against me, and I forgive him? As many as seven times?" Jesus answers, "No, seventy times seven!" (Matt. 18:21–22). Then Jesus relates a parable about a king to illustrate the nature of forgiveness (Matt. 18:23–35). The king wanted to settle accounts with his debtors. One man brought before him owed the king a staggering sum of ten thousand talents, which in today's currency would run into the tens of millions of dollars.[1] Antipas' annual revenue from both Galilee and Peraea was only two hundred talents.[2] So the man's debt was astronomical and he had no possibility of ever paying it. The king commanded that he, along with his wife and children and all his possessions, be sold and partial payment made. This judgment was consistent with the legal practice stipulated in the Mosaic law (Exod. 22:3; cf. Neh. 5:4–5; Amos 2:6; 8:6).[3] Confronted with the horror of this prospect, the debtor broke down and begged, "Lord, have patience with me, and I will pay you everything."

Touched with pity at the man's undone condition, the king ignored the incredulous promise to pay all and ordered that the huge debt be canceled. But no sooner had the forgiven servant left the king's presence than he ran into a fellow servant who owed him a relatively small sum, a mere hundred denarii. He throttled the poor fellow, demanding immediate payment in full. His fellow servant's plea echoed his own words, "Have patience with me, and I will pay you." The forgiven man refused and put his debtor in prison until he paid off his debt.[4]

When word reached the king of this heartless deed done by the servant that he had so graciously forgiven, the king summoned his ungrateful servant and angrily chided him. "You wicked servant!" he said, "I forgave you all that debt because you besought me; and should not you have had mercy on your fellow servant, as I had mercy on you?" Then the king condemned the man to the torturers until he paid his debt or until death freed him. The parable concludes with the admonition and the warning, "So also my heavenly Father will do to every

National Geographic photographic tower.

one of you, if you do not forgive your brother from your heart."[5]

Jesus' parable concerning the kingdom of heaven is set in the king's accounting office in a great banking center, like the city of Sepphoris. The king, representing the heavenly Father, is a figure of sovereignty possessing vast wealth and unchallenged power. His control of large financial transactions creates the potential for both making and losing large fortunes. When his servant is hopelessly unable to pay, the king first commands that the law be enforced and that the man be sold, with his family and possessions, and partial payment made. But, the king is not obligated to exact strict legal justice; he is free to show mercy and to forgive the debt. This he does!

When the forgiven servant fails to appreciate the magnitude and the significance of the king's generosity, the king can and does reverse his initial act of mercy and fully expresses his wrath. The parable is reminiscent of the idea stated in the Lord's Prayer: "For if you forgive men their trespasses, your heavenly Father also will forgive you; but if you do not forgive men their trespasses, neither will your Father forgive your trespasses" (Matt. 6:14). The bottom line—to use an accounting term—is, "Be merciful, even as your Father is merciful" (Luke 6:36).[6]

The Parable of the Pounds

As Jesus approaches Jerusalem shortly before his crucifixion, he tells another parable about a king. A nobleman goes to a distant land to obtain a kingdom. But, his enemies send an embassy close on his heels to protest his appointment.[7] Nevertheless, he becomes king and returns in power to his own country. Then he commands that his enemies be brought into his royal presence and executed (Luke 19:12, 14, 15, 27).

While the basic events outlined in this parable are rather general, some have seen in it an allusion to Archelaus' (Antipas' full brother) bid to become king following the death of Herod the Great. Archelaus sailed to Rome in 4 B.C. hoping to be appointed king by Augustus. A Jewish delegation followed him from Judea, however, and protested.[8] When Archelaus returned to Judea as ethnarch and with the promise of becoming king should he rule well, he did not forget his old enemies. With great brutality he hunted them down, executed them, and confiscated their property. Deposed and exiled by Augustus in A.D. 6, the memory of Archelaus' brutal reign long outlived him.[9]

This parable depicts the king's absolute life and death power over his subjects. At his return he will execute judgment on those who dare to oppose his rule. Not knowing when he will come again, the course of wisdom is to remain loyal and faithful until he returns with kingly might at the second coming.

Interwoven with this parable concerning the king's return is another in which the nobleman, before leaving to seek his kingdom, calls in ten of his servants (Luke 19:12–27; cf. Matt. 25:14–30).[10] To each he gives a pound (about fifty dollars), with the instruction that they trade with them until he returns. After an extended absence, the nobleman, now king, comes back and summons his servants. The first with the pound entrusted to him had accrued an additional ten. The king commends him with enthusiasm. "Well done, good servant! Because you have been faithful in a very little, you shall have authority over ten cities." The second servant had earned five more pounds. He too is commended by the king and rewarded with the administration of five cities.

The third servant hesitantly approaches the king and unfolds a napkin in which he had carefully kept the king's pound. He blames the king for his own fear and indolence.[11] "I was afraid of you," he confesses, "because you are a severe man; you take up what you did not lay down, and reap what you did not sow." The king rebukes his slothful servant. "Why then did you not put my money into the bank, and at my coming I should have collected it with interest?" Then the king gives the irresponsible servant's pound to the servant who had demonstrated the most ability. And the king observes, "I tell you, that to every one who has will more be given; but from him who has not, even what he has will be taken away."

In this parable the king's unpredictable arrival conveys an implicit warning to be prepared. Those entrusted with his resources must stand and render an account of their dealings. They are challenged to be industrious and faithful until that day of reckoning comes, when the king returns with full authority demanding to settle all accounts. The image of a sovereign king and the mention

Marble fragments.

of a bank paying interest suggest a cultural milieu similar to the capital at Sepphoris or Tiberias.[12]

The Parable of the King's Wedding Feast

Matthew attributes a parable to Jesus that compares the kingdom of heaven "to a king who gave a marriage feast for his son" (Matt. 22:1–3, 11–14).[13] Royal preparations for the young prince's wedding would be elaborate. The invited guests are the most important and influential people of the realm and neighboring lands. When all things are ready, the king sends servants to all those previously invited. The servants announce, "Come, for the wedding feast is beginning!"

As the guests arrive, dressed appropriately for such an auspicious nuptial celebration, they enter the great hall, where according to custom spices thrown on a fire emit a pleasant odor that lightly scents the vast chamber. Numerous brightly burning lamps cast a soft yellow glow over the large tables laden with bounties of rich foods and succulent delicacies: roast beef, fresh breads, dates, raisins, almonds, walnuts, and honey-sweetened cakes. Excellent wine flows freely as the rejoicing overflows to the sounds of music and dancing. The groom receives the congratulations of the guests and his young bride is adorned and adored.

Suddenly in the midst of the festivities the king appears, dressed in his royal purple robe. He moves among his guests, nodding and with reassuring smiles acknowledging their presence.[14] Then the king spies a man not properly dressed for this royal wedding. The king singles him out and asks, "Friend, how did you get in here without a wedding garment?" Stunned speechless, the man makes no excuse. "Bind him hand and foot," the king orders his attendants, "and cast him into the outer darkness; there men will weep and gnash their teeth."

The appearance of the king focuses attention on the significance of what may be understood as the great messianic wedding feast. The king inspects those guests in attendance and determines if their attire is suitable for the matrimonial celebration. His uncontested judgment is severe and challenges the hearers of this parable to array themselves in robes of righteousness as preparation for that time of appraisal.[15]

Associated with Matthew's version of the parable about the king's wedding feast for his son is the parable of a great feast.[16] As soon as the wedding banquet is prepared, the king sends his servants to convey his formal invitation to the guests. The servants even recite the items on the menu. But, the invitees do not take the king's invitation seriously; one goes off to his farm while another attends to business. Others abuse the servants and kill them. Enraged at those who have spurned his gracious invitation, the king commands his army to attack and burn their cities and to slaughter the murderers.

Now the king turns to his servants and observes, "The wedding is ready, but those invited were not worthy." He decides to throw open the doors of his banquet hall to all his subjects. To his servants he says, "Go therefore to the thoroughfares, and invite to the marriage feast as many as you find." The servants obey and the wedding hall is filled with a great throng, both good and bad.

In this parable concerning the kingdom of heaven, the king prepares a great marriage celebration but his invited guests fail to attend. Their rejection of the present opportunity to participate in the messianic wedding feast brings down the king's hot anger, for they cannot ignore the sovereign's gracious invitation with impunity. He vents his wrath by unleashing the full might of his military to annihilate his enemies. Some in the early church doubtless saw in this parable an allusion to the destruction of Jerusalem in A.D. 70 but those Galileans who first heard it could call to mind the destruction of Sepphoris in 4 B.C.[17]

Those who snubbed the king's initial invitation are punished and he extends his offer to all who will joyfully share in the festivities of his son's messianic nuptials. The challenge to the hearer is to respond with gratitude and joy to the king's magnanimous welcome.

Jesus' Teaching on the Cost of Discipleship

A king makes another appearance in a saying of Jesus that stresses counting the cost of discipleship (Luke 14:25–33). A large crowd follows after Jesus and he turns and says, "If any one comes to me and does not hate his own father and mother and wife and children and brothers and sisters, yes, and even his own life, he cannot be my disciple. Whoever does not bear his own cross and come after me, cannot be my disciple."

Jesus emphasizes the need to calculate the radical cost of being his disciple. Who would begin to construct a tower without carefully estimating the total expense of construction? If one lays the foundation and then realizes that he cannot complete construction, the foundation becomes a monument to inadequate planning.

Jesus asks what king contemplating a war against another king would not first counsel with his military strategists to determine if with ten thousand soldiers he could repel an attack, although outnumbered two to one. If his army is judged to be inadequate and defeat is likely, the king will commission an embassy to negotiate a peace treaty.[18]

It is noteworthy that Jesus makes this specific reference to a king planning a military campaign. Given the strategic location of Galilee and Peraea, which served as a buffer between Rome and both the Parthian Empire and the Nabataean kingdom, Antipas was preoccupied with his military strength. In typical Herodian fashion and with considerable success, he sought to stabilize his realm with a strong and efficient army. When Aretas, the Nabataean king, routed Antipas' army in the autumn of A.D. 36, the defeat was due to treachery rather than weakness. So impressive was Antipas' huge military build up that Agrippa, his brother-in-law, successfully accused him before the Roman emperor of plotting sedition. Antipas confessed that he had stockpiled a large store of weapons and was sent into exile.[19]

Jesus' parable reflects an awareness of the military planning and preparation that kings must continually make to secure themselves against aggression. Jesus encourages his followers to be circumspect, to count the cost, and to be willing to pay the price that the security of God's kingdom requires. "So therefore, whoever of you does not renounce all that he has cannot be my disciple" (Luke 14:33).

The Temple Tax

After beginning his public ministry, Jesus moves his residence from Nazareth to Capernaum on the north shore of the Sea of Galilee, where Simon Peter lived. The Gospel of Matthew (17:24–27) contains the story of some tax collectors who come from the Jerusalem temple and inquire if Jesus pays the half-shekel temple tax. Collected annually from male Jews, the voluntary tax was a sign of loyalty and support of the Jerusalem temple worship.[20] Peter answers, "Yes."

When Peter returns home, Jesus questions him. "What do you think, Simon? From whom do kings of the earth take toll or tribute? From their sons or from others?" Capernaum was near the border toll station where Levi, or Matthew, collected taxes before becoming a disciple of Jesus. "Tribute" apparently refers to the poll tax paid annually to Antipas' government. Jesus is criticized by his enemies for being a friend of tax collectors and sinners, who would be able to provide him with firsthand knowledge of Antipas' pervasive tax system.

The phrase "kings of the earth" implies a higher heavenly kingship. Central to Jesus' message is the proclamation of the nearness of the kingdom of God and the necessity of accepting and acknowledging God's sovereignty over all of creation. Psalms sung in the temple praised Yahweh as King of his people and indeed the earth. Yahweh is enthroned upon the praises of Israel. "Lift up your heads, O gates! and be lifted up, O ancient doors! that the King of glory may come in. Who is this King of glory? The LORD of hosts, he is the King of glory!" (Ps. 24:9–10). As children of the Great King and citizens in his heavenly kingdom, Jesus and his brethren could be considered exempt from the obligation to pay the temple tax. This theological perspective on freedom would not be fully appreciated by those officials appealing for funds to underwrite temple expenditures. As the leader of a religious revival movement, Jesus' refusal to contribute to the temple would expose him to unnecessary and unwarranted criticisms (see Mark 12:13–17 and parallels). So Jesus tells Peter to pay the half-shekel.

Peter is instructed to cast a hook into the sea and catch a fish; from its mouth he is to take a shekel and with the coin pay the temple tax for both Jesus and himself. This is the only mention in the New Testament of fishing with a hook.[21]

An interesting footnote to this story has been provided by excavations at Capernaum by the Franciscans. Beneath a fourth- or fifth-century octagonal Byzantine church they uncovered a first-century house, tentatively identified as the house of Peter. Graffiti on the walls—scratched by pilgrims in Aramaic, Syriac, Latin, and Greek—mention Peter and express prayers to Jesus. Underneath the floor of the house fishhooks were discovered.[22]

Jesus' Teaching on Power

On one occasion James and John, the fishermen sons of Zebedee, ask Jesus to grant them a special request (Matt. 20:20–28; Mark 10:35–45; Luke 22:24–27). Jesus inquires, "What do you want me to do for you?" And they reply, "Grant us to sit, one at your right hand and one at your left, in your glory." They are anxious to share power and authority when the kingdom becomes fully established. But Jesus asks if they are prepared to share also in his sufferings as well as his power, if they are willing to "drink the cup" and "accept the baptism" that he must endure. They respond, "We are able." They will indeed share his sufferings, Jesus tells them, but to sit beside him in power is not his to grant.

We are reminded of another occasion when a similar argument arose among the twelve (Matt. 18:1–5; Mark 9:33–37; Luke 9:46–48). Aware that they disputed over who is the greatest, Jesus calls them and says, "If any one would be first, he must be last of all and servant of all." Then Jesus places a child in their midst. He holds the child in his arms as he says, "Whoever receives this child in my name receives me, and whoever receives me receives him who sent me; for he who is least among you all is the one who is great" (Luke 9:48).

The ten other apostles, who had overheard James' and John's self-serving request, are angry. Then Jesus explains to the twelve the nature of real authority in the kingdom of God. "The kings of the Gentiles exercise lordship over them; and those in authority over them are called benefactors" (Luke 22:25).[23] Jesus shows a knowledge of kings and political rulers whose arbitrary authority often led to cruel and abusive use of power. These kings frequently assumed the title "benefactor"—especially in Syria and Egypt—as a claim of good deeds performed for the state.[24]

In the new regime that Jesus proclaims leadership and greatness will be measured by the capacity and performance of loving service. "Let the greatest among you become as the youngest, and the leader as one who serves." The true "benefactor," like Jesus, is the person who best ministers to human needs. "For which is the greater," he asks, "one who sits at table, or one who serves? Is it not the one who sits at table? But I am among you as one who serves" (Luke 22:27; cf. Matt. 10:24; Luke 6:40; John 13:12–17).

The kingdom of God announced by Jesus and the movement that he launched is destined to clash with established economic, political, and religious institutions. This tension grows during Jesus' ministry and continues for those who exalted him as Lord. In their distress, his disciples could take some comfort in imitating his sufferings as they accepted and affirmed the reign of God over all creation.

In an apocalyptic passage predicting the coming trials and tribulations that the community must endure, Jesus warns his disciples that numerous false leaders will arise and lead many astray. There will also be international conflicts (wars and rumors of wars) and natural disasters (earthquakes and famines). In addition to these chaotic events, his followers will be brought before councils, will be beaten in synagogues, and will stand before governors and kings to testify of their faith in Jesus and the kingdom of God. Peace and security will be lacking even at home, for enmity will prevail between parents and children and among siblings (Matt. 10:16–23; Mark 13:3–13; Luke 21:10–19).

Kings in this apocalyptic saying represent high political power protecting and preserving the past with its institutions and values. These old forms are challenged by the vision of the heavenly kingdom that Jesus proclaims. Earthly kings may judge the disciples and sentence them accordingly, but the faithful will endure in the firm conviction that they serve a higher King. "But he who endures to the end will be saved" (Mark 13:13).

In the final judgment scene described in Matthew 25:31–46, the Son of man arrives as a great king. He appears as a supernatural figure, coming in glory with his angelic entourage.[25] Sitting on his majestic throne, the king pronounces judgment upon all the nations gathered before him. He separates those assembled into the redeemed and damned, like a shepherd divides the sheep from the goats. This motif of separating the good from the bad is characteristic of Matthew and can be observed in the parables about wheat and chaff (3:12), broad and narrow roads (7:13–14), wise and foolish builders (7:24–27), wheat and tares (13:24–30), good and bad fish (13:47–50), two sons (21:28–32), prepared and unprepared guests (22:11–14), and wise and foolish maidens (25:1–13).[26]

The basis for the king's judgment astonishes both the righteous and the wicked. To those on the right he says, "Come, O blessed of my Father, inherit the kingdom prepared for you from the foundation of the world" (Matt. 25:34). The criteria for this joyous welcome are deeds of humanitarian service— not obedience to religious rituals or conformity to legal regulations. The king continues, "I was hungry, thirsty, a stranger, naked, sick, and imprisoned, and you ministered to my needs." Surprised and grateful for this unexpected commendation, the righteous inquire, "Lord, when did we see you so and minister to you?" Then the king answers, "Truly, I say to you, as you did it to one of the least of these my brethren, you did it to me."

The king turns and curses those on the left and with a crushing sentence consigns them to the "eternal fire prepared for the devil and his angels." When confronted with people in need, the wicked had been indifferent and apathetic. They protest, "Lord, when did we see you in need and fail to respond?" And the king answers, "As you did it not to one of the least of these, you did it not to me."

In this vision of the end time, the eschaton, the apocalyptic king comes in awesome power to judge, reward, and punish all nations. But even now he is present incognito in the everyday needs of people that call out for compassion and active attention. The weak, helpless, and undesirable provide the opportunity to render loving service—not just to these unfortunates but through them to the Great Monarch whose sovereignty extends over all humanity. His judgment pronounced upon the sheep and goats is final. The eternal fire will not be redemptive and those entering there abandon all hope. But, the vision of hell is redemptive for those who yet have time to accept the full meaning of the kingdom of God.[27]

The references to kings in the parables and sayings attributed to Jesus in the Gospels suggest that his cultural horizons are far wider than those of a remote Galilean village. The image of king points consistently to the concept of the king's sovereignty over his subjects. He determines their economic fortunes, freedom and slavery, and life and death. The king's judgments at times are harsh and exacting and at others tempered with mercy but his authority is never successfully challenged. Such an understanding of kingship may well reflect an awareness of Antipas' rule from Sepphoris and Tiberias. Antipas' appointment as king, or tetrarch, came directly from Rome and he represented the vast power of the empire in his territories. Jesus skillfully employs the figure of the king as an unquestioned authority to point toward God's sovereignty over creation and to challenge his disciples with the seriousness of life in the dawning kingdom of God.[28]

Herod Antipas' Galilean Economy

There was a rich man, who was clothed in purple and fine linen and who feasted sumptuously every day. And at his gate lay a poor man named Lazarus, full of sores, who desired to be fed with what fell from the rich man's table; moreover the dogs came and licked his sores. (Luke 16:19–21)

Antipas' Galilee was a relatively rich and productive land that generated great wealth for a privileged few while many struggled just to survive. There were the rich upper class and the peasants, with few between.[1] Josephus' somewhat overstated description of the land points to the basis for a flourishing economy: "For the land is everywhere so rich in soil and pasturage and produces such variety of trees, that even the most indolent are tempted by these facilities to devote themselves to agriculture. In fact, every inch of the soil has been cultivated by the inhabitants; there is not a parcel of waste land."[2]

Galilee in Jesus' day was small, with an area of about 750 square miles. It measured approximately thirty miles north to south and twenty-five miles east to west. Bordering Samaria on the south and Phoenicia on the west and north, Galilee's eastern border followed the course of the Jordan River. It began at Lake Huleh and continued south through the Sea of Galilee and along the Jordan River. East of this border were the territories of Gaulanitis and the Decapolis.

The hills of Galilee rise in the north (Upper Galilee) to over 3,300 feet.[3] The broad valleys in the south (Lower Galilee) have rich soil able to produce a variety and abundance of crops. Annual rainfall in the north averages forty inches, somewhat less in the south. Galilee remains today a fertile and productive land. In Antipas' day Galilee supported a population estimated at 200,000, living mostly in small farming villages.[4] Sepphoris, according to Josephus, was the largest city in Galilee, boasting a population estimated at between 25,000 and 30,000. When, as the Gospels say, "Jesus went about all the cities and villages," he would not have traveled far between them (Matt. 9:35; Mark 6:6, 56), for Josephus claims that there were 204 cities and villages in Galilee.[5]

Sepphoris dominated a high hill that afforded a view northward across the wide and fertile Bet Netofa Valley. This lush green valley was the bread basket for the capital and a major factor in the selection of this site for the city. Food produced locally could feed the large and growing population without the difficulty of transportation.

The mild Mediterranean climate, with wet winters and hot dry summers, was ideal for growing grains, grapes, and olives, basic to the diet.[6] Agriculture was attuned to the annual natural cycle. Fall cereals were planted at the

The
market at
Sepphoris.

beginning of the rainy season in late October or early November and grew until after the rains ended in late March. In spring and early summer the grain matured until golden and ready for the sickle.[7] From the city one could look over the wall and see the growing grain on which the life of the capital depended. Jesus' parable about a sower would be familiar to both urbanites and peasants.

The sower, with a sack of seeds slung across his shoulder by a sturdy strap, strides across the newly ploughed field scattering the grain in measured and rhythmic motions. His pace quickens as he watches the dark rain clouds drifting in from the Mediterranean. Some seeds fall on the hardened path, where the birds eat them. Others fall on rocky ground and quickly grow but later wither and die. Still others fall among thorns and are choked. Some seeds fall on the fertile soil and yield thirty, sixty, and one hundredfold (Matt. 13:3–9; Mark 4:3–9; Luke 8:5–8). Drawing on a scene from daily life, Jesus explains how the word of God that he broadcasts is being hindered by the devil, shortlived enthusiasm, and the desire for riches and pleasure. But, those disciples who accept the kingdom of God and live in its power will be a productive force in society and bring forth an abundant harvest of faith and love.

Agriculture drove the economy of Galilee—wheat and barley ground and baked into bread, grapes pressed for wine or dried as raisins, oil squeezed from olives used in cooking and cosmetics. A variety of vegetables contributed toward a more balanced diet, such as beans, lentils, and onions. Plump succulent figs and delicious dates from the palm groves near the Sea of Galilee added a sweet touch to the table. Almonds and walnuts were plentiful, tasty, and nourishing.

Flax, flourishing in the mild wet winters and hot summers, produced a thriving linen industry centered in Sepphoris.[8]

Roman pottery from Sepphoris.

Forested hillsides mantled with tall, straight, and sturdy oaks, pines, and walnut trees provided timber and fuel. Olive trees and cedars also supplied wood for crafts.

On a walking tour around Galilee, Jesus and his disciples saw numerous shepherds pasturing their sheep and goats on the spring grasses and flowers, soon to be burned brown in the heat of summer. Sheep produced thick wool, which was spun into thread and woven into warm cloth. Young lambs became meat for food. Goats' milk was especially nutritious and could be turned into a strong tasting cheese. Skins were tanned and used for many purposes, from writing materials to carrying water.

Although cattle were relatively expensive and inefficient to raise, the wealthy grazed select herds in the deep grasses and ate tender veal from calves fattened in the stalls. The cattle produced an enviable supply of milk, butter, cheese, and hides. On the road one encountered docile donkeys plodding patiently beneath their heavy burdens. A herd of fine horses, employed in Antipas' fast-moving cavalry, feed on one of his royal estates. Mules transport men and materials; oxen strain to pull loaded wagons over the rough road. Occasionally one must step aside for a camel caravan to pass, coming from the trade routes in Peraea and Nabataea, its precious and exotic cargo bound for the capital of Sepphoris or the port of Ptolemais.

Pigs, raised for Roman appetites and sacrificial rites, remind one of Rome's pervasive influence.

Fishing in the Sea of Galilee was another important industry in Antipas' Galilee. Jesus' apostles—Peter, Andrew, James, and John—actively engaged in this profitable occupation. Fresh fish taken with nets from the clear blue waters were sold the same day in the markets of nearby towns and villages. Some fish were cleaned, salted, dried, or pickled and then sold in more distant Galilean markets or exported.

Tomatoes grown in the Bet Netofa Valley.

The major center of this commercial fishing enterprise was the town of Magdala or Magdal Nunia, from the Hebrew word meaning "fish tower." It was given the Greek name *Tarichaeae,* because of the large quantities of salted and pickled fish it exported.[9] Located on the western shore of the Sea of Galilee about five miles north of Tiberias, Magdala was also the home of Jesus' close friend Mary Magdalene, from whom Luke says Jesus exorcised seven demons (Luke 8:2).

Josephus indicates that although the lake abounded with fish, competition was stiff, because 230 boats were working on the Sea of Galilee.[10] The lake measures 13 miles by 7 miles; its surface is 680 feet below the level of the Mediterranean. This freshwater lake is fed by the snows that melt on Mount Hermon and Mount Lebanon and gush up as cold crystal clear springs near Caesarea Philippi.

In January 1986, a two-thousand-year-old boat was found on the western shore of the Sea of Galilee, a short distance north of Magdala.[11] This amazing discovery has yielded fascinating new information about life on the lake as Jesus knew it. A severe drought in 1985 and early 1986 caused the level of the lake to drop drastically, exposing a broad shelf of lakebed. In the mud, the oval outline of a boat protruded. Shelley Wachsmann, inspector of Underwater Antiquities for Israel's Department of Antiquities, made a preliminary examination of the boat and concluded that it was ancient. How ancient he could not tell immediately. Just as Shelley investigated the boat a sudden rain shower was followed by a beautiful double rainbow, that he took to be a sign of the potential importance of the discovery.

Racing against time, Shelley hastily organized an excavation team comprised largely of volunteers. He was concerned that the boat might be destroyed by treasure hunters seeking the gold rumors said it contained. The excavation began on February 16 and continued around

Two-thousand-year-old hull of boat.

the clock for eleven days. Heavy winter rains ended the long drought and the lake began to rise rapidly, threatening to inundate the entire project. But, the Kinneret Authority that manages the lake arrived just in time to build an earth and sand bag dike to hold back the encroaching water.

Volunteers meticulously removed by hand the mud encasing the boat. Gradually its ancient form emerged. The boat measured twenty-six and a half by seven and a half feet. Exposed to the air, the boat was in imminent danger of drying out and disintegrating. Orna Cohen, a conservator at Hebrew University, devised a brilliant but untested plan to preserve the fragile vessel. First, she reinforced the boat with a frame of fiberglass and polyester and wrapped it in sheets of plastic. Then she sprayed it with polyurethane foam that soon hardened into a protective cocoon.

The boat was floated and pushed through an opening cut in the dike to a point on shore just north of the discovery site. A crane lifted the boat, shell and all, into a specially constructed pool. Removed from its protective cover, it will soak in a synthetic wax solution for about five years, until the wax replaces the water in the wood. Hardened by this slow process, it will be placed on permanent display in the Yigal Allon Museum at Kibbutz Ginnosar.[12]

Carbon-14 dating of ten samples of wood taken from the boat has dated its construction to 40 B.C., plus or minus eighty years. A careful investigation of its size, shape, and construction determined that it was a working vessel, probably a fishing boat comparable to that used by the apostles. In fact, a first-century mosaic, found at Magdala and now on display at Capernaum, depicts a similar boat. Normally the boat carried a crew of four oarsmen and a helmsman who steered with a rudder. There was originally a mast supporting a single sail.[13]

About the time Jesus began his ministry, he moved to Capernaum, less than four miles from where this boat was discovered. Jesus as a skilled carpenter may have worked on this type of vessel. The Gospels tell that he traveled, slept, and taught in just such a boat. As the excavations continued for several days, the volunteers sought comic relief from the strain of long hours, cold, and fatigue. Shelley told me that one volunteer was overheard joking, "This boat is large enough to carry thirteen passengers but there were only twelve seats. One must have had to walk on the water."

The discovery of this first-century boat adds vivid details to some of the stories told about Jesus. Once as he was teaching on the shore, the people crowded around him. Two fishing boats anchored there were empty, because the fishermen were washing their nets after the long night's work. Jesus stepped into one of the boats and pushed out a little way from the shore, sat down, and taught the people (Luke 5:1–3).

Mosaic from Magdala.

After the lesson, Jesus said to Simon Peter, "Put out into the deep and let down your nets for a catch." Peter protested wearily that they had been fishing unsuccessfully all night, but did as instructed. When the net was hauled in, it began to tear from the great weight of the catch. Peter called out to his partners, James and John, to bring the other boat. The large catch swamped both boats so that they were in danger of sinking. All were overwhelmed and overjoyed at their belated success, but Peter knelt before Jesus and confessed, "Depart from me, for I am a sinful man, O Lord." To which Jesus replied, "Do not be afraid; henceforth you will be catching men" (Luke 5:4–11).

Land in Galilee was the primary source for generating income and wealth. Antipas owned large royal estates inherited from his father, Herod the Great.[14] Some of these rich lands were located, no doubt, in the fertile Bet Netofa Valley just north of his new capital at Sepphoris. An ample and dependable food supply was essential for Antipas' administration: food for the government officials responsible for banking and the regulation of markets; food for those charged with the oversight of domestic and foreign trade, the keeping of records, and the collection of taxes. Food was essential for the standing army as well as for additional Roman legions that would arrive to put down rebellion. Food was needed for construction workers who were working on the new city's construction projects. Sepphoris was built almost entirely from local raw materials that cost Antipas nothing—stones quarried on the site, trees cut for beams and lumber, clay for roof tiles. (Much marble was imported.) Food was necessary for slaves, day laborers, artisans, and architects.[15]

Tribute to Rome was paid with grain. In a dry year, when the winter rains were few and brief and crops did not grow, a surplus store of grain could ward off famine and rebellion, stabilize domestic consumption, and provide seeds for the fall planting.

If the production of an abundant supply of grain and other food stuffs was essential to Antipas' rule, the ability to preserve them was equally important. The key to the preservation of grain was to store it in a secure dry place protected from the winter rains and bandits. Sepphoris as the fortified capital near the Bet Netofa Valley was an important city for the storage of Antipas' grain.

Large plastered underground chambers discovered on the top of the acropolis at Sepphoris have been tentatively identified as silos as well as cisterns.[16] In 1985 I borrowed the National Geographic Society's ground-penetrating radar to assist in our archaeological excavations at Sepphoris. After training at the manufacturer of the radar, Geophysical Survey Systems, I shipped the radar to Israel. Carolyn, my wife, and I adjusted the radar to the conditions of the soil on the site at Sepphoris and investigated several subsurface features prior to the excavation.

In one area the radar printout indicated that subterranean chambers were hidden beneath approximately five feet of dirt and debris and another six feet of bedrock. Finding no access, it was decided to probe straight down into the chambers, in spite of the potential hazard of a ceiling collapse. When our team had dug a six-foot-square probe to bedrock, we found a three-foot-round hole chiseled through the solid bedrock. The ancient chamber beneath had filled during the intervening years with sand, dirt, and fragments of pottery. We carefully cleared away the fill to discover a large smoothly plastered room cut in the shape of a round jug. The circular chamber measured approximately sixteen feet in diameter and fifteen feet from the floor to the opening at the top. At the level of the floor an arch four feet high led into an identical empty chamber three feet away. These chambers originally were cut down from the surface and then connected by a low arched passageway before being plastered. Then the chambers were filled with either grain or water and all but one of the openings to the surface sealed.

More cisterns and silos discovered on the site demonstrate a basic concern to provide the city with ample water as well as food for any eventuality, whether siege or famine.

In addition to Antipas' royal estates, government officials, members of the nobility, and wealthy priests or Sadducees farmed large tracts of productive land. Many of this wealthy class resided in the cities, like Sepphoris and Tiberias, and rented their lands to tenants.[17] Rents and taxes were exorbitant, and tenants earned a marginal income that in a bad season could prove financially devastating. But, without land of his own the tenant farmer was bound economically to the land and his landlord.

Some of Jesus' parables reflect this social situation. One tells of a man who planted a vineyard on some choice acreage, protected it with a thick hedge, and erected a tall tower to keep watch over the ripening grapes. He dug a pit for the wine press. Then he rented his vineyard to tenants and left them to carry on their viticulture. When harvest came, the landlord sent one of his servants to collect the rent—payable in grapes, raisins, or new wine. The tenants, however, beat the servant and drove him off empty-handed. The second servant the tenants abused, striking him on the head. The third they killed. Other servants they likewise shamefully mistreated. Finally, the unbelievably patient landlord sent his own beloved son in the misguided hope that the tenants would respect him and pay the past due rent. But, they murdered the son as well, plotting to seize the vineyard once the heir was dead. "What will the owner of the vineyard do?" Jesus asks his audience. Then he answers that the landlord himself will come with sufficient force to destroy the abusive tenants and the vineyard will be leased to others (Matt. 21:33–43; Mark 12:1–12; Luke 20:9–18).

This parable strikes a familiar theme in Jesus' teaching concerning the need to be watchful and responsible as a disciple in the kingdom of God. It also sheds light on a familiar economic pattern, where well-to-do landlords, owning valuable real estate and making significant capital investments, lease their vineyards or farms to tenants, who are expected to be industrious and fiscally responsible. The landlord anticipates a sizable profit from his investments.

In another parable Jesus compares the kingdom of heaven to a man hiring day laborers to work in his vineyard (Matt. 20:1–16). At sunrise he agrees with some workers in the marketplace to pay them the customary wage of one denarius for a full day's work and sends them off to his vineyard. In mid-morning, the owner returns and finds other workers idle in the market. He tells

Cistern at Sepphoris.

them also to go and work in his vineyard and he will pay them a fair wage. Trusting, they go. At noon and in mid-afternoon, the owner of the vineyard employs still others to join in the harvesting. Finally, only an hour before quitting time, the man discovers some unemployed laborers and asks, "Why do you stand here idle all day?" They reply, "Because no one has hired us." These too are hired and put to work.

When evening comes the workers gather around the owner's steward to collect their wages. The paymaster begins with those hired last—at the eleventh hour—and gives them a denarius as though they had worked all day. Those laborers hired first expect to be paid extra but they also receive only a denarius. One complains to their employer, "These last worked only one hour, and you have made them equal to us who have borne the burden of the day and the scorching heat." The owner of the vineyard responds, "Friend, I am doing you no wrong; did you not agree with me for a denarius? Take what belongs to you, and go; I choose to give to this last as I give to you." And he adds, "After all, it's my money! Why criticize my generosity?"

Jesus' parable comes to focus on a radical theology of reversal, for when the kingdom arrives "the last will be first, and the first last" (Matt. 20:16). The parable assumes a familiar economic situation where wealthy landowners hire day laborers, who work long and hard in the fields and vineyards for a subsistence wage. Jesus does not criticize the owner of the vineyard nor commend the laborers. In fact, the owner is represented as fair in the management of his business and even capable of generosity. But the land and the money are his and the workers are dependent on his resources and discretion.

Once while Jesus is teaching, a voice comes from the crowd, "Teacher, bid my brother divide the inheritance with me" (Luke 12:13). Jesus declines to become embroiled in either a sibling or a civil conflict. "Guard

Boys in the marketplace.

against covetousness," Jesus warns. Covetousness is proscribed in the Ten Commandments. A person is valuable because of what he is rather than what he has. Jesus tells his audience about a wealthy farmer who one year had a bumper crop. Unable to store the bountiful harvest, he looked across his fields of golden grain and wondered what to do and decided to raze his old barns and build larger ones. Anticipating his financial security and well-earned retirement, he muses on the time soon when he can sit back and say to himself, "You have ample goods laid up for many years. Eat, drink, and be merry!" But, God says, "Fool! Tonight you die. Then whose harvest will this be?" Greed feeds on insecurity. The farmer apparently is industrious and shrewd in the management of his business but is not rich toward God. The parable depicts a wealthy class with large fields under cultivation and driven by a profit motive and greed. They think security will be gained through amassing personal wealth. Then comes the Grim Reaper!

The economic contrast between rich and poor is underscored in Luke's parable about a rich man (called Dives, from the Latin word used in the Vulgate to translate the Greek adjective "rich") and a poor man named Lazarus (Luke 16:19–31). In the opening scene Dives, dressed in royal purple and fine linen, resides in a beautiful house and enjoys excellent cuisine. Just outside the gate of his courtyard, Lazarus, a poor infected beggar, lays and eats the scraps from Dives' table. Dogs lick Lazarus' sores. Both men die. The scene changes drastically as angels carry Lazarus to rest in Abraham's bosom; Dives arrives in Hades, tormented in the flames. Seeing Lazarus' repose, Dives cries out to Abraham to have mercy and to send Lazarus with a single drop of water to cool his parched tongue. Abraham replies that Dives must remember their former circumstances, when he was at ease and Lazarus was in misery. Now the tables are turned and their conditions unalterable. Not easily silenced, Dives pleads with

Abraham to send Lazarus to warn his five brothers of the agony awaiting them. But, Abraham also refuses this request, pointing out that the brothers have the law and the prophets to instruct them. "If they do not hear Moses and the prophets," Abraham says, "neither will they be convinced if some one should rise from the dead" (Luke 16:31). This parable dramatically contrasts the great disparity between the rich and poor and provides insight into the prevalent economic situation in Jesus' Galilee.

Between the extremes of rich and poor in Galilee, however, lived many peasants farming small plots of fertile land. Living in the more than two hundred villages that dotted the countryside, these independent and industrious farmers earned a modest income to support their families and shouldered a major portion of Galilee's tax burden. While not organized into a political unit, these peasants, if confronted with a threat to their traditional religious values, could act in concert and exert tremendous pressure on the ruling authorities.

Josephus tells of an interesting and informative episode when in A.D. 39 the Roman emperor Gaius gave the order to erect his statue in the Jerusalem temple.[18] Other nations had built temples to honor the emperor as a divine ruler. Gaius commanded Petronius, the governor of Syria, to march on Jerusalem and set up the emperor's statue. If Petronius met armed resistance, he was to crush it with force. Petronius quartered his troops at the port of Ptolemais for the winter, fully intending to march on Jerusalem in the spring. At Ptolemais a delegation of tens of thousands of Jews petitioned Petronius not to commit this sacrilege against their temple. Next, Petronius rode to Tiberias to assess the situation and was met by an even larger number of Jews protesting the proposed erection of Gaius' statue. They said that they would not fight the Roman legions and would accept death rather than acquiesce in this violation of the Mosaic law. Then they fell down and bared their throats to the Romans' swords.

As this protest continued for forty days, the Galilean farmers abandoned their fields and neglected the fall planting. This "sit down strike" was in danger of creating a widespread famine and producing no crops with which to pay next year's taxes.

Word of the volatile and potentially tragic showdown in Galilee reached King Agrippa, who was in Rome paying court to the emperor. Agrippa, who at that time ruled Galilee, skillfully convinced Gaius to rescind his order to Petronius and thereby averted a terrible disaster for the Jewish nation.[19]

This interesting account from Josephus demonstrates the political and economic influence of the independent peasant farmers and the importance of their produce for the health of the Galilean economy. Jesus' parable of the prodigal son may depict the life-style of these peasant farmers (Luke 15:11–32).[20]

The father in the parable has two sons. The younger asks for the share of property coming to him and the father divides his living between his two boys. Soon the younger goes far from home and squanders his money. Forced by hunger to take the unenviable job of feeding pigs, his thoughts turn homeward. At home even his father's hired servants have more than enough to eat. When the young man, penniless and penitent, returns home, his father warmly welcomes him and tells the servants, "Bring quickly the best robe, and put it on him; and put a ring on his hand, and shoes on his feet; and bring the fatted calf and kill it, and let us eat and make merry; for this my son was dead, and is alive again; he was lost, and is found" (Luke 15:22–24).

The elder brother arrives later from working in the fields and hears music and dancing in the house. Inquiring of a servant about the celebration, the servant tells him that his younger brother has arrived unexpectedly and his father is throwing a party for him. The older son refuses to join in the merriment; the father comes out to encourage his first born to participate in the celebration. The elder son complains. "For years I have worked hard and been obedient and you have not given me so much as a kid to celebrate with my friends. But, when this immoral and irresponsible son of yours shows up, you slaughter the fatted calf and make a great celebration." "Son, you are always with me," the father responds patiently, "and all that is mine is yours. It was fitting to make merry and be glad, for this your brother was dead, and is alive; he was lost, and is found."

Jesus' parable of the prodigal son held up a mirror to the hundreds of peasant farmers living in Galilee. The farmer in the parable has his sons working in the fields with the hired servants. His house is large enough to accommodate a joyful celebration with plentiful food, music, and dancing. He has a calf fattened in the stall for a special event. Flocks of sheep and goats graze on marginal land. Combined with Antipas' royal estates and the large tracts of land cultivated by the nobility and aristocracy, the independent and industrious peasant farmers produced considerable prosperity for Galilee.[21]

7

The Economy of the Kingdom of God

Fear not, little flock, for it is your Father's good pleasure to give you the kingdom. Sell your possessions, and give alms; provide yourselves with purses that do not grow old, with a treasure in the heavens that does not fail, where no thief approaches and no moth destroys. For where your treasure is, there will your heart be also. (Luke 12:32–34)

On the sabbath soon after Jesus begins his public ministry, he attends the modest synagogue in his own small village of Nazareth (Luke 4:16–23). The attendant takes the large scroll of Isaiah from the cabinet or ark where it is kept and hands it carefully to Jesus. Jesus stands at the lectern and by the natural light of day unrolls the scroll to its innermost section. Then he reads from the Hebrew text (Isa. 61:1–2) as those assembled listen reverently to the words of the great prophet. "The Spirit of the Lord is upon me, because he has anointed me to preach good news to the poor. He has sent me to proclaim release to the captives and recovering of sight to the blind, to set at liberty those who are oppressed, to proclaim the acceptable year of the Lord" (Luke 4:18–19). When Jesus returns the scroll to the attendant and sits down, all eyes are focused on him. Then Jesus begins to interpret the significance of the prophecy in the light of his own ministry, "Today this scripture has been fulfilled in your hearing" (Luke 4:16–21). With these provocative words, Jesus announces the arrival of a new age in which the poor, handicapped, confined, and oppressed will be liberated.[1]

Jesus launches his renewal movement in Galilee with an aggressive preaching tour, traveling "about all the cities and villages, teaching in their synagogues and preaching the gospel of the kingdom, and healing every disease and every infirmity" (Matt. 9:35; cf. 4:23; 11:1; Mark 6:6, 56; Luke 13:22). The Gospel accounts of Jesus' travels are sketchy. Sepphoris, according to Josephus, the largest and most influential city in Galilee, may well be included in this general description.[2] Antipas would view any popular leader with suspicion. As Jesus' acclaim grew, Sepphoris would be a precarious setting for his proclamation of the arrival of the kingdom of God.[3]

Sepphoris, the capital of Galilee and Peraea from approximately the time of Jesus' birth until he began his public ministry, flourished as the center of government and finance. Resident within Sepphoris' strongly fortified walls, many wealthy court officials carried out Antipas' political and fiscal policies. Landlords rented out their land holdings and reaped lucrative returns; merchants engaged in profitable trade both at home and abroad; and prosperous businessmen amassed large fortunes through shrewd transactions.[4] Antipas' economy, accord-

Synagogue.

ing to the Gospels and Josephus, was fueled by greed and the desire for financial security.[5] Associated with wealth's power and prestige was the desire for ease and luxury, when one could say, "Soul, you have ample goods laid up for many years; take your ease, eat, drink, be merry" (Luke 12:19). These profits, derived in large measure from the exploitation of slaves, tenants, and peasants, provided the material wealth for the privileged upper class.

Jesus announced to those whose lives were bound up with Antipas' political and economic system that a new day was dawning—the arrival of the kingdom of God. Antipas was deeply disturbed by reports of Jesus' growing popularity and his preaching, which clearly sowed the seeds of radical change and signaled a potential revolution.[6] Jesus stood in sharp contrast to those Jewish apocalyptists whose vague visionary language predicted the coming of God's kingdom at some remote future age. Such bizarre forecasts, devoid of specific programs for implementation, might be tolerated by Antipas' government. But Jesus proclaimed that God's kingdom was at hand and that his ministry was itself a sign that a new day was dawning. "But if it is by the finger of God that I cast out demons, then the kingdom of God has come upon you" (Luke 11:20). Although the kingdom's inception may go unnoticed by many, it will soon grow, like leaven in dough or a tiny grain of mustard seed planted in the ground, and produce astonishing results. Jesus told his audience, "Truly, I say to you, there are some standing here who will not taste death before they see the kingdom of God come with power" (Mark 9:1; cf. Matt. 16:28; Luke 9:27).[7]

Asked by some Pharisees when God's kingdom would arrive, Jesus' response resonated with a sense of urgency. Although immanent, the kingdom could not be located in a specific place, "for behold, the kingdom of God is in the midst of you" (Luke 17:21).[8] Jesus was reluctant to set an exact time for the coming of God's reign and informed his followers, "But of that day or that hour no one knows, not even the angels in heaven, nor the Son, but only the Father. Take heed, watch; for you do not know when the time will come" (Mark 13:32–33; cf. Matt. 24:36).

God is the Creator and Sustainer of all life. This message is at the center of Jesus' proclamation of the kingdom or reign of God. Faith in God's sovereignty, benevolence, and nearness demands radical obedience.[9] The disciple may no longer measure the value of life by material possessions if he is not rich toward God (Luke 12:15, 21).

Once as Jesus started out on a journey, a rich young Jewish ruler ran up to him and knelt down asking, "Good Teacher, what must I do to inherit eternal life?" Jesus deflects his praise, saying that no one is good except God, and then proceeds with an answer. "You know the commandments: 'Do not kill, Do not commit adultery, Do not steal, Do not bear false witness, Do not defraud, Honor your father and mother." The man responds that he has observed all these commandments from his early youth. Jesus looks lovingly at the man and offers a challenge and an enviable invitation: "You lack one thing; go, sell what you have, and give to the poor, and you will have treasure in heaven; and come, follow me." Deeply sorrowful and pained by Jesus' challenge, the man left, "for he had great possessions." In spite of, or perhaps because of his wealth, the radical cost of discipleship was too high (Mark 10:17–22; cf. Matt. 19:16–22; Luke 18:18–24). This young ruler's love for his wealth prevents him from receiving the "treasures in heaven" that Jesus promises. His greed typifies many Galileans confronted by Jesus' proclamation of the kingdom of God.[10]

Aware of those standing by, Jesus adds a warning: "How hard it will be for those who have riches to enter the kingdom of God!" Indeed, a camel can pass through the eye of a needle more easily than a rich man can enter the kingdom (Mark 10:23–25).[11] But those, who for the sake of Jesus and his gospel, forsake family, lands, and houses, will receive a hundredfold in this life (although with persecutions) and eternal life (Mark 10:29–31; cf. Matt. 19:29–30; Luke 18:28–30).[12] The primary issue is one of loyalty and trust. "No one can serve two masters; for either he will hate the one and love the other, or he will be devoted to the one and despise the other. You cannot serve God and mammon" (Matt. 6:24; Luke 16:13). Jesus' emphasis is also found in the Ten Commandments. "You shall have no other gods before me!" the first commandment stipulates. The second proscribes granting to anything within creation the worship due the Creator alone (Exod. 20:3–6; Deut. 5:7–10).

Attempts to discover life's meaning and purpose within creation, the material world, lead to anxiety and insecurity. Those anxious about their food and clothing should learn a lesson from the birds and flowers.[13] "Look at the birds of the air," Jesus says, "they neither sow nor reap nor gather into barns, and yet your heavenly Father feeds them. Are you not of more value than they?" (Matt. 6:26). The lilies growing in the fields do not toil or spin and yet God arrays them in natural splendor greater even than Solomon's glory (Matt. 6:28–29). God clothes the green grasses of spring that tomorrow will burn to heat an oven. Will he not also provide adequate protection for those trusting in him? (Matt. 6:30). Jesus claims that in God's creation not a single sparrow falls to the ground without God's will. Even the hairs of one's head are numbered (Matt. 10:29–30; Luke 12:6–7). "Fear not, therefore." Worrying about life's basic necessities, such as food and clothing, distracts the disciple from the source of genuine existence and will not add to the length of life—indeed, anxiety may subtract from both life's longevity and joy.

What then is the disciple to do? "But seek first his kingdom and his righteousness, and all these things shall be yours as well" (Matt. 6:33).[14] The surprise and joy of entering the kingdom is like that of a man who finds a treasure hidden in a field and sells everything in order to purchase the field. To put God's kingdom foremost is comparable to a pearl merchant who discovers a single exquisite pearl and sells all he has and purchases it (Matt. 13:44–45). To focus one's being on the solitary goal of God's kingdom is to discover life's true meaning. "The eye is the lamp of the body. So, if your eye is sound, your whole body will be full of light" (Matt. 6:22; Luke 11:34).

Jesus expresses his radical ethic in the commands, "Be merciful, even as your Father is merciful" (Luke 6:36) and "You, therefore, must be perfect, as your heavenly Father is perfect" (Matt. 5:48). Trusting fully in God's sovereign love, the disciple shares this love with others and so reflects the divine nature in interpersonal relationships.[15] Faith in God's care liberates the disciple from the tyranny of material possessions and "the cares of the world." The person of faith becomes free to respond to human needs wherever they are encountered. In a loving response he shares God's spirit of compassion. "And whoever gives to one of these little ones even a cup of cold water because he is a disciple, truly, I say to you, he shall not lose his reward" (Matt. 10:42; Mark 9:41).

Jesus teaches that God, the source of all good gifts, responds graciously to the disciples' prayer requests. He instructs his followers to pray, "Give us this day our daily bread" (Matt. 6:11; Luke 11:3). Who among you, Jesus inquires of his audience, if his son asks for bread or a fish would give him a stone or a serpent? "If you then, who are evil, know how to give good gifts to your children, how much more will your Father who is in heaven give good things to those who ask him!" Then Jesus sums up his admonition: "So whatever you wish that men would do to you, do so to them; for this is the law and the prophets" (Matt. 7:11–12; Luke 6:31).

If someone begs or asks to borrow something, the disciple should readily grant the request. God's gifts are bestowed freely on those who do not merit them. "For he makes his sun rise on the evil and on the good, and sends rain on the just and the unjust" (Matt. 5:45; cf. Luke

6:34–35). So Jesus' disciples are to do deeds of loving-kindness for those who may neither claim nor deserve them and from whom no repayment may be expected. Such is the quality of mercy. "But when you give a feast, invite the poor, the maimed, the lame, the blind, and you will be blessed, because they cannot repay you. You will be repaid at the resurrection of the just" (Luke 14:13–14).

Jesus rejects the popular doctrine of retribution that claimed a person's condition or station in life was a direct result of God's approval or disapproval. Those Galileans whom Pilate slaughtered at their sacrifice were no worse than other Galileans. The eighteen men crushed beneath the tower of Siloam were not different from others living in Jerusalem (Luke 13:1–5).[16] Human tragedy and suffering are not invitations to find fault and place blame but rather an opportunity to perform acts of kindness and humanitarian service. A person's true worth is determined by God's unmerited favor revealed in the ministry of Jesus and not by meritorious or self-righteous deeds.

Once while Jesus is teaching a crowd, a lawyer stands up and puts him on trial with the question, "Teacher, what shall I do to inherit eternal life?" (Luke 10:25). Jesus, acknowledging the man's expertise in the Mosaic law, responds, "What is written in the law? How do you read?" The lawyer answers astutely, capturing the essence of the Mosaic law by combining two passages from the Pentateuch (Deut. 6:5; Lev. 19:18). "You shall love the Lord your God with all your heart, and with all your soul, and with all your strength, and with all your mind; and your neighbor as yourself." Actually, his answer is not unlike that given on another occasion by Jesus himself (Matt. 22:34–40; Mark 12:28–34) and even other contemporary Jewish teachers. Jesus commends the lawyer for his insight and the precision of his excellent answer. "You have answered right; do this, and you will live" (Luke 10:28).

The lawyer, however, "desiring to justify himself," seeks to determine the limits of his liability, through defining

Roman lamp.

the extent of his neighborhood. He wants to distinguish between those who might legitimately lay claim to his concern and those for whom he needs to feel no affection. So he inquires, "And who is my neighbor?"[17]

Jesus answers, not with a legal definition of "neighbor," but with a parable. A certain man, a Jew, traveling down the road from Jerusalem to Jericho, through the barren and forbidding hills of Judea, was overpowered by robbers. They beat him, stripped him, and abandoned him half-dead beside the road. First a priest and next a Levite, a member of the priestly tribe, passed the man, noticed his pitiful condition, and yet ignored him. Then a Samaritan, a foreigner with whom many strict religious Jews were reluctant to deal, came along the road and had mercy on his fellow man. This Samaritan, a persona non grata in Judea, knelt down, and poured oil and wine on the man's wounds and bandaged them. Then the Samaritan carried the unfortunate man on his own beast to an inn and personally cared for him through the night. The next morning before the Samaritan departed, he gave the innkeeper two denarii and instructed him to provide for the injured man while he recuperated and then promised to pay the bill upon his return.

Then Jesus asks the lawyer to pronounce his own judgment. "Which of these three, do you think, proved neighbor to the man who fell among the robbers?" "The one who showed mercy on him" comes the obvious reply. "Go," Jesus says, "and do likewise." The lawyer had begun with an attempt to justify himself by circumscribing the limits of his neighborhood and establishing the point beyond which he had no responsibility. Where, he seems to ask, does the obligation to love end and can I ignore human suffering and need? Jesus leads the lawyer to an understanding that is basic to life in the kingdom of God. A loving person will express genuine compassion whenever and wherever a fellow human being is in want.[18]

The arrival of the kingdom that Jesus proclaims will bring with it a radical change in the economic and social order of Antipas' realm. Instead of trusting in riches and greedily accumulating wealth, Jesus encourages his disciples to share their possessions in order to alleviate suffering and to satisfy human needs. Jesus often criticizes the wealthy who have hoarded large fortunes and are indifferent toward the weak and poor around them.[19] Dives and Lazarus, the rich farmer who planned to build larger barns in which to store his bountiful harvest, and even the parable of the Good Samaritan carry forth the responsibility to show mercy.

The rich in Jesus' parables are anxious to protect their great possessions from being stolen. He tells about a fully armed man, no doubt a rich nobleman, who guards his palace, where he has secured his possessions (Luke 11:21). No one can ravage a strong man's house, Jesus points out, unless they first tie him up. Only then can the robbers steal his goods (Matt. 12:29; Mark 3:27). Jesus compares a scribe, trained for the kingdom, to a householder who brings from his treasure room valuable antiquities and newly acquired wealth (Matt. 13:52).[20] Amassing vast fortunes in a land where the majority live near poverty means that the wealthy must be on guard against thieves. The need for constant vigilance is expressed by Jesus' warning that if the householder had known when during the night to expect the thief, he would stay at home and remain alert (Matt. 24:43; Luke 12:39).

Against the greed and avarice that Jesus witnesses, he challenges his audience to open a secure account in which to deposit their most precious treasures. "Do not lay up for yourselves treasures on earth, where moth and rust consume and where thieves break in and steal, but lay up for yourselves treasures in heaven, where neither moth nor rust consumes and where thieves do not break in and steal. For where your treasure is, there will your heart be also" (Matt. 6:19–21).

Jesus teaches that surprising and even revolutionary changes in existing conditions will characterize the arrival of the kingdom of God. He affirms a theology of reversal and envisions a future radically different from present expectations.[21] At Capernaum, where Jesus made his home after leaving Nazareth, a centurion comes to him. The centurion, a Gentile officer commanding a hundred soldiers and in the service of Herod Antipas,[22] tells Jesus that his servant is seriously ill, paralyzed and in terrible distress. Jesus volunteers to go and heal the sick man but the centurion protests, saying that he is not worthy for Jesus to enter his house. He asks only that Jesus say the word, believing that alone sufficient to heal his servant. Jesus is pleasantly surprised at the centurion's great faith and says to those standing by, "Truly, I say to you, not even in Israel have I found such faith." Then Jesus predicts that in the kingdom it will be drastically different from what one might anticipate. "I tell you, many will come from east and west and sit at table with Abraham, Isaac, and Jacob in the kingdom of heaven, while the sons of the kingdom will be thrown into the outer darkness; there men will weep and gnash their teeth." Then Jesus turns to the centurion and grants his request in accordance with the centurion's faith (Matt. 8:5–13; Luke 7:1–10).[23]

The theme of reversal and the turning of the tables colors many of Jesus' teachings. He reminds those in Nazareth familiar with the Elijah and Elisha stories that it was the widow at Zarephath in Phoenicia whom Elijah fed during a severe famine. It was not an Israelite but Naaman, commander of the Syrian army, that Elisha cleansed of the dreaded leprosy (Luke 4:24–30). The first will be last, and the last first (Matt. 20:16; Mark 10:31; Luke 13:30). To his closest followers Jesus warns against grabbing for power; "let the greatest among you become as the youngest, and the leader as one who serves" (Luke

Tomb at Sepphoris.

22:26; cf. John 13:13–16). "Whoever seeks to gain his life will lose it, but whoever loses his life will preserve it" (Luke 17:33).

Jesus tells his disciples when they attend a wedding feast not to sit in a place of honor lest they be asked to move and surrender the seat to a more important guest. The disciples should occupy a humble place from which their host may invite them to move up. "For every one who exalts himself will be humbled, and he who humbles himself will be exalted" (Luke 14:11; cf. 18:14; Matt. 23:12).[24]

The emphasis on reversal in Jesus' teachings creates a dramatic impact on his listeners, who are consistently challenged by the unexpected outcomes. The Samaritan, not the priest or the Levite, cares for the seriously wounded Jew beside the road. The prodigal son, not the self-righteous elder brother, provides the occasion for the father's elaborate celebration. Lazarus, not the rich man, enjoys the comfort of Abraham's bosom. The rich farmer's untimely death destroys his dream of a long and luxurious retirement.

The idea of an economic revolution is also integral to Jesus' message about the kingdom. The revolution will not arrive by a violent overthrow of the established order, but by compassion redefining the appropriate use of wealth.[25] "Give to every one who begs from you; and of him who takes away your goods do not ask them again. And as you wish that men would do to you, do so to them" (Luke 6:30). "But love your enemies, and do good, and lend, expecting nothing in return; and your reward will be great, and you will be sons of the Most High; for he is kind to the ungrateful and the selfish" (Luke 6:35). "Give, and it will be given to you; good measure, pressed down, shaken together, running over, will be put into your lap. For the measure you give will be the measure you get back" (Luke 6:38).

The Gospel of Luke is especially concerned with the plight of the poor and oppressed. Jesus promises them that in the kingdom their lives will be enriched. "Blessed are you poor," Jesus proclaims to the great throng assembled to hear him on the plain, "for yours is the kingdom of God. Blessed are you that hunger now, for you shall be satisfied. Blessed are you that weep now, for you shall laugh" (Luke 6:20–21; cf. Matt. 5:3–4, 6). These blessings are counter-balanced by woes pronounced against the well-to-do. "But woe to you that are rich, for you have received your consolation. Woe to you that are full now, for you shall hunger. Woe to you that laugh now, for you shall mourn and weep. Woe to you, when all men speak well of you, for so their fathers did to the false prophets" (Luke 6:24–26).[26]

It is no wonder that the common people hear Jesus gladly and that the rich and powerful, along with Antipas, view Jesus' growing popularity with suspicion and fear (Mark 12:37; Luke 9:7). Jesus instructs the rich to use the power of their wealth to minister to the poor and suffering. Both rich and poor are encouraged not to make material possessions the measure of their worth before God. The rich focus on their wealth and the poor on their needs; both must acknowledge that a merciful Father is the source of all true life and live in the full joy of this realization.

Poverty is not an excuse for failing to be merciful. At the temple in Jerusalem, Jesus sits across from the treasury and watches people making their contributions. Many rich donate large sums. Then a poor widow comes and places two tiny copper coins into the treasury. Jesus tells his disciples that her small gift was more generous than the larger sums because "she out of her poverty has put in everything she had, her whole living" (Mark 12:41–44; Luke 21:1–4). Even the poor can express mercy.[27]

The Gospels portray Jesus as envisioning a new economy in sharp contrast to the greed, avarice, and exploitation characterizing Antipas' economic system. In a word,

Jesus calls for a redistribution of wealth as a means of sharing and expressing God's compassion for all his creation. The wealthy, resident in Sepphoris and throughout Galilee, could only view with alarm the rapidly growing popularity of Jesus' renewal movement.

Jesus, Friend of Tax Collectors

And Levi made him a great feast in his house;
and there was a large company of tax
collectors and others sitting at table with them.
And the Pharisees and their scribes murmured
against his disciples, saying, "Why do you eat
and drink with tax collectors and sinners?"
And Jesus answered them, "Those who are
well have no need of a physician, but those
who are sick; I have not come to call the
righteous, but sinners to repentance."
(Luke 5:29–32)

fter Jesus concludes teaching a crowd gathered near the Sea of Galilee, he walks the road along the northern shore. About two miles east of Capernaum, where Jesus had made his new home, the road crosses the Jordan River, which marks the boundary between Antipas' Galilee and Herod Philip's territory. Near this border crossing, Levi sits at a tax office collecting tolls for Antipas' government from the numerous travelers, merchants, and caravans coming into Galilee.[1] Jesus walks up to Levi and says, "Follow me." Levi leaves his post and follows. He must have heard about Jesus' ministry around the sea and responds immediately to the opportunity to be his disciple. At this busy tax office there are other tax officials, no doubt, and some of Antipas' police (Matt. 9:9; Mark 2:13–14; Luke 5:27–28).

Soon Levi prepares a great feast in his house, which is spacious enough to accommodate a large number of tax collectors, who attend and recline at the tables with Jesus, his disciples, and other guests.[2] Levi's ability to give an expensive feast in his own home, providing good food and ample wine, suggests that he had profited from collecting taxes. There is no mention, however, that his considerable income had been derived dishonestly. The scene is one of conviviality, where many, considered to be sinners in respectable religious circles, respond gladly to the invitation to join in the feasting. They participate in the fellowship and atmosphere of celebration with their host and Jesus. To eat with people in this society implies acceptance and friendship.[3] Jesus joins fully in the festivities.

On another occasion, Jesus commends the tax collectors for their genuine comradery and observes, "For if you love those who love you, what reward have you? Do not even the tax collectors do the same?" (Matt. 5:46). Jesus appreciates the fellowship enjoyed by the tax collectors and the affection that they share, an affection based largely on common values and circumstance. Jesus calls his own disciples to a love and compassion that reflect the divine character of God as Father. He encourages his disciples, "You, therefore, must be perfect, as your heavenly Father is perfect" (Matt. 5:48).[4]

Levi's generosity and hospitality in giving this feast, as well as the numerous guests who attend, indicate his influential standing in the community, especially among his professional colleagues. In such a comfortable setting, one might easily learn about Antipas' tax system. The conversations may have touched on various aspects of their business. How contracts for collecting taxes were obtained at the capitals of Sepphoris or Tiberias. Which were the most lucrative businesses or districts. How to extract the maximum amount of money from the people.

Seeing Jesus feasting and fellowshipping with tax collectors, the Pharisees and their scribes complain to Jesus' disciples. "Why," they ask indignantly, "do you eat and drink with tax collectors and sinners?" These self-appointed guardians of the Jews' religious traditions express a resentment of tax collectors shared by a majority of Galileans. Jesus overhears their criticism and responds, "Those who are well have no need of a physician, but those who are sick; I have not come to call the righteous, but sinners to repentance" (Matt. 9:12; Mark 2:17; Luke 5:31–32).

The tax collectors, themselves Jews, extorted exorbitant taxes, estimated at more than 30 percent, from their fellow countrymen for a government kept in power by Rome.[5] They were hated primarily because of their dishonesty in squeezing oppressive taxes from the people, for they pocketed any money collected in excess of the amount set down in their contracts. Tax collectors were excluded from much of respectable Jewish society. When the Gospel of Matthew speaks of disfellowshipping a sinful member from the church, Jesus says, "Let him be to you as a Gentile and a tax collector" (Matt. 18:17).[6]

Matthew, named among the twelve apostles, is identified as a tax collector (Matt. 10:3) and is a knowledgeable source of information for Jesus about Antipas' tax system.[7] Jesus' frequent and familiar associations with tax collectors establish his reputation as their friend. In keep-

Roman-style
bath house.

Coin from Sepphoris.

ing with his theology of reversal, Jesus tells the religious authorities at the temple, "Truly, I say to you, the tax collectors and the harlots go into the kingdom of God before you" (Matt. 21:31).

The tax collectors whom Jesus befriends are in the service of Antipas' government.[8] They comprise a small army of bureaucrats who receive their commissions from the capital at Sepphoris and later at Tiberias. They extort money from every profitable sector of the flourishing economy. Antipas inherited an efficient, lucrative, and oppressive tax system from his father, Herod the Great.[9] While much specific information concerning his tax structure is lacking, it is possible to sketch a reliable picture from information gleaned from Josephus, the Gospels, and ancient tax policies in the Middle East. Antipas, the "fox," knew well how to exploit fully the natural and human resources of Galilee and Peraea.

Herod Antipas' Tax Structure

Galilee was strategically located near major trade routes. The highway from Damascus in Syria to ports on the Mediterranean Sea ran northeast of the Sea of Galilee to the capital of Sepphoris. From Sepphoris a road led northwest to the coastal city of Ptolemais. Another major roadway went southwest from Sepphoris to Caesarea Maritima and continued along the coastal plain to Egypt.[10] Not far south of Sepphoris a branch of this main road ran south through Samaria and then on to Jerusalem. Tolls collected from travelers, merchants, and caravans using this system of roads provided substantial revenues for Antipas' treasury. Levi worked for Antipas' government, collecting tolls at the border crossing of the Jordan River just north of the Sea of Galilee.

Galilee's soil was fertile and the annual rainfall in most years ample for a variety of crops. Antipas' own royal estates, located in the rich Bet Netofa Valley north of Sepphoris, were efficiently managed and worked many slave laborers. Antipas rented other royal lands to friends and wealthy aristocrats, whose annual payments contributed substantially to the royal coffers. The tax on royal lands was an effective means of controlling the nobility in Galilee.[11] Taxes could be adjusted as a means of rewarding or punishing "friends of the crown" (cf. Mark 6:21).[12] Some payments were made in grain and other food supplies and were stored in strategic locations.

Land taxes on the numerous small farms of the industrious Galilean peasants added to the government's revenues.[13] At harvest, when the peasant with his entire family gathered the wheat, barley, olives, grapes, and flax, Antipas' tax collectors appraised the produce and separated the king's share. Antipas' forty-two-year reign was a peaceful one that allowed his realm to prosper.[14] He provided his subjects peace and security and exacted high taxes in return—but not so high as to inflame a revolt. As long as Antipas could maintain the peace, he might avoid the fate of his brother, Archelaus, who in A.D. 6 had been removed by Augustus as ethnarch in Jerusalem because of riots.[15]

Antipas' government also controlled fishing rights in the lakes and streams.[16] When fishermen, such as Peter, Andrew, James, and John, had fished all night and docked early in the morning with their fresh catch, Antipas' tax collectors were waiting.

Herod the Great had placed a tax on public purchases and a sales tax on agricultural produce and other commodities.[17] Antipas apparently continued this policy. When a farmer brought his produce to sell at the public market in a city or town, he could expect to pay a tax on the food sold. The local commissioner of markets, whose responsibility was to regulate weights and measures as well as prices, cooperated with the tax collectors in exacting the sales tax. Antipas appointed Agrippa, the brother of his wife, Herodias, to be commissioner of markets in the new city of Tiberias. Agrippa did not like the job or the pay and quit.[18] A thirty-six-ounce lead weight unearthed in 1985 at Sepphoris reveals the name of a local market inspector, a Jew named "Simon son of Aianos son of Justus."[19]

Antipas also collected an annual poll tax from every male subject fourteen to sixty-five years old.

Augustus set Antipas' annual personal income at the generous sum of two hundred talents.[20] Additional amounts were expended on tribute to Rome, public works projects, the construction of Sepphoris and Tiberias, and Antipas' costly military buildup. Antipas' minister of finance, Chuza, monitored fiscal policy and the complicated tax system, noting the appointments of tax collectors and seeing that the amounts stipulated in their contracts were promptly paid. Detailed records of all important assignments and transactions were kept safe at the archives in Sepphoris and Tiberias.[21]

Tax Collectors in the Ministry and Teachings of Jesus

Once after speaking of John the Baptist, who was being held in prison by Antipas, Jesus addresses the crowd and contrasts his own style of ministry with that of John. The people of this generation, Jesus complains, are like children sitting in the marketplace, calling out to their playmates, who are reluctant to play any games. "We piped to you, and you did not dance; we wailed, and you did not weep."[22] Then Jesus tells his audience, "For John the Baptist has come eating no bread and drinking no wine; and you say, 'He has a demon.' The Son of man has come eating and drinking; and you say, 'Behold, a glutton and a drunkard, a friend of tax collectors and sinners!' Yet wisdom is justified by all her children" (Luke 7:32–35; cf. Matt. 11:17–19).

John the Baptist's call to repentance had been well received by some tax collectors who reportedly believed John's message (Matt. 21:32), received his baptism (Luke 3:12), and praised God (Luke 7:29). When these penitents inquired of the ascetic prophet what they should do, John's answer was direct and simple, "Collect no more than is appointed you." After John's arrest, Jesus' renewal movement gains momentum and the tax collectors accept his message of forgiveness and hope for the kingdom of God.

Luke tells of an occasion when tax collectors and sinners draw close to hear Jesus. The Pharisees and scribes stand back and watch, repeating their criticism, "This man receives sinners and eats with them" (Luke 15:1–2).

In response, Jesus relates three parables that treat something lost and found and the joy that accompanies the recovery.

Jesus asks his audience, "What man of you, having a hundred sheep, if he has lost one of them, does not leave the ninety-nine in the wilderness, and go after the one which is lost, until he finds it?" Relieved, the shepherd returns home carrying the sheep on his strong shoulders and shouts to his friends and neighbors, "Rejoice with me, for I have found my sheep which was lost." Then Jesus says for all to hear, "Just so, I tell you, there will be more joy in heaven over one sinner who repents than over ninety-nine righteous persons who need no repentance" (Luke 15:7).[23]

Then Jesus asks, if a woman has ten silver coins and loses one, would she not light a lamp and carefully sweep the floor of her house to find it? Once she has discovered the lost coin, she invites in her neighbors saying, "Rejoice with me, for I have found the coin which I had lost." Jesus concludes to a grateful group of tax collectors, "Just so, I tell you, there is joy before the angels of God over one sinner who repents" (Luke 15:10).[24]

The third parable concerns the prodigal son who takes his inheritance and wastes it in a foreign country. When poverty forces him to return home, he expects to become as one of his father's household servants. Instead, his father warmly welcomes him and celebrates his son's return with a great feast, music, and dancing. The older brother, who had always stayed at home and worked, would not join in the merriment. The father goes out to him in order to include him in the festivities. The audience understands this parable as an invitation to those on the fringe of respectable society to enter joyfully into the kingdom of God. The parable also conveys God's offer to include the self-righteous who will repent and join in the messianic celebration (Luke 15:11–32).[25]

On his last trip to Jerusalem shortly before his crucifixion, Jesus journeys down the Jordan River to the ancient city of Jericho. Herod the Great had built his opulent winter palace near Jericho and cultivated the lucrative date palm and balsam groves. As Jesus passes through the city, word of his coming precedes him and a large crowd gathers and moves along with him through the streets. Zacchaeus, a chief tax collector, wishes to see Jesus but Zacchaeus is short and cannot see over the heads of the crowd. Casting aside formalities in his eagerness to see Jesus, Zacchaeus climbs into a sycamore tree (a type of wild fig tree). From his perch, he looks down and watches Jesus passing. Jesus notices Zacchaeus' intense curiosity and calls up to him, "Zacchaeus, make haste and come down; for I must stay at your house today." Joyfully Zacchaeus climbs down and escorts Jesus to his fine home. Some in the crowd are overheard murmuring, "He has gone in to be the guest of a man who is a sinner." Zacchaeus was rich, for he was a chief tax collector in the employ of the Roman prefect, Pontius Pilate, appointed by the government of the emperor Tiberius. As a tax officer with other collectors working for him, Zacchaeus had become wealthy in the important frontier post of Jericho.[26]

Jesus talks with Zacchaeus about life in the kingdom and Zacchaeus is profoundly touched and convicted by Jesus' words. Then Zacchaeus volunteers, "Behold, Lord, the half of my goods I give to the poor; and if I have defrauded any one of anything, I restore it fourfold." Jesus is pleased with his generous offer and assures Zacchaeus that his investment will be well placed. "Today," Jesus promises, "salvation has come to this house, since he also is a son of Abraham. For the Son of man came to seek and to save the lost" (Luke 19:9–10).

Jesus detects in many tax collectors an awareness of sin and spiritual need that leads them to genuine sorrow. He tells a parable "to some who trusted in themselves that they were righteous and despised others" (Luke 18:9).[27] A tax collector and a Pharisee went into the magnificent temple in Jerusalem, built by Herod the Great. "The Pharisee stood and prayed thus with himself," informing God of his own righteous life and thanking God that he was superior to others—"extortioners, unjust, adulterers, or even like this tax collector." Just to be sure, the Pharisee tells God that he fasts two days of every week and gives a tithe of his gross income.

In marked contrast, the tax collector stands to one side with downcast eyes and beats his breast. Overwhelmed with remorse he expresses his solitary petition, "God, be merciful to me a sinner!" The tax collector, Jesus says, will go home justified in God's sight rather than the self-righteous Pharisee. Both were Jews but one acknowledged his deep need for God's forgiveness and with a broken heart laid claim to God's mercy. Then Jesus faces his shocked audience and affirms again his theology of reversal, "for every one who exalts himself will be humbled, but he who humbles himself will be exalted" (Luke 18:14).[28]

During the week before Jesus' crucifixion in Jerusalem, some Pharisees and Herodians attempt to entrap him with a question about taxes. The Herodians are considered to be loyalists of the Herodian family and in favor of paying Roman taxes.[29] The Pharisees, an influential Jewish religious sect, debated the issue. These two different groups join forces in putting this dilemma before Jesus (Matt. 22:15–22; Mark 12:13–17; Luke 20:20–26).

They begin with disarming flattery. "Teacher, we know that you are true, and care for no man; for you do not regard the position of men, but truly teach the way of God." Then they pose their trick question: "Is it lawful to pay taxes to Caesar or not? Should we pay them, or should we not?" The specific tax in question is probably the poll tax (*tributum capitis*) levied on all male subjects of Rome between the ages of fourteen and sixty-five. The principle of the payment of Roman taxes, however, was much broader.

The question of whether to pay Roman taxes had been a burning issue in Galilee. Josephus states that during the procuratorship of Coponius (A.D. 6–9), a Galilean named Judas "incited his countrymen to revolt, upbraiding them as cowards for consenting to pay tribute to the Romans and tolerating mortal masters, after having God for their lord."[30] The resentment of Roman taxation continued to smolder in Galilee and flared up on several occasions. If Jesus advises against paying taxes, these spies could easily "deliver him up to the authority and jurisdiction of the governor," Pontius Pilate. On the other hand if Jesus, known to be a friend of tax collectors, counsels others to pay taxes to Rome, he will jeopardize the support of many followers in both Galilee and Judea who are opposed to Roman domination.[31]

Jesus, well aware of the dilemma presented to him, asks to see a coin. His opponents hand him a silver denarius stamped with the profile of the Roman emperor Tiberius. By being in possession of this coin, they tacitly acknowledge their acceptance of the Roman presence and control. The coin bearing Caesar's image was in violation of the strict interpretation of the second commandment, proscribing idolatry and the making of any graven images. Jewish coins of this time did not display a human face.[32]

Jesus holds up his opponents' silver denarius, worth approximately a day's wage, and inquires, "Whose likeness and inscription is this?" They respond in unison, "Caesar's." Then Jesus amazes them with his penetrating answer: "Render to Caesar the things that are Caesar's, and to God the things that are God's." Their either/or question had been based upon the false assumption that the payment of taxes to Caesar and faithfulness to God were incompatible. But, Jesus' reply points out that the Roman coin struck with the emperor's image should rightly be paid back to him, while a human being made in God's image should belong wholly to God.[33]

Jerusalem,
City of the
Great King

"Nevertheless I must go on my way today and tomorrow and the day following; for it cannot be that a prophet should perish away from Jerusalem." O Jerusalem, Jerusalem, killing the prophets and stoning those who are sent to you! How often would I have gathered your children together as a hen gathers her brood under her wings, and you would not!
(Luke 13:33–34)

Spring arrives cool and clear in Galilee. Passover draws near. Jesus sets his face toward Jerusalem (Luke 9:51), determined to proclaim the kingdom of God in the Holy City and accept the painful consequences (Matt. 16:21; Luke 18:31). The winter rains are ending; the bright blue sky hosts white billows; hills are alive with varying shades of green and sport a riot of colors from the fresh flowers. Shepherds tend their flocks. The flax harvest is ending and the barley will soon be cut. It is a season for pilgrimages.

Jesus makes his journey to Jerusalem along the Jordan River, swollen with the winter rains and racing along its serpentine course toward the Dead Sea. At Jericho, some 1,200 feet below the level of the Mediterranean Sea, he turns west and climbs the steep ascent toward Jerusalem 18 miles away and 2,500 feet above sea level.

When Jesus reaches the summit of the Mount of Olives, near the villages of Bethany and Bethphage, he can see across the deep green olive groves, the Garden of Gethsemane, and the Kidron Valley to Mount Zion and the massive eastern fortification walls of Jerusalem. Above these walls rises Herod the Great's magnificent temple. "O Jerusalem, Jerusalem." Jesus reflects upon a city rich with traditions and the center of Jewish faith and practice, a city that has witnessed great accomplishments as well as devastating and tragic defeats. This Holy City is the setting for the final act of Jesus' ministry.

Jesus instructs two of his disciples to go to one of the villages, where they will find a colt that had never been ridden (Mark 11:1–10). "Untie it and bring it," he says. The two find the colt and are untying it when some bystanders challenge them. The disciples respond that the Lord needs it but will return it shortly. They lead the colt to Jesus and place their outer tunics on its back. Jesus sits on the colt and begins the two-mile ride down the Mount of Olives and up to Jerusalem.

Pilgrims throng the road in a festive mood as they approach the Holy City to celebrate the passover and recall God's mighty acts of the Exodus. Caught up in the charged atmosphere filled with hope and expectation, the people cut branches and lay them on the road and spread their garments along the way for Jesus to ride over. They begin a chant reminiscent of Psalm 118:26, a psalm of praise and promise traditionally sung at passover.

"Hosanna! Blessed is he who comes in the name of the Lord! Blessed is the kingdom of our father David that is coming! Hosanna in the highest!" (Mark 11:9–10).

Luke (19:39–44) tells of some Pharisees in the crowd who immediately sense the potential danger of this enthusiastic demonstration, with its possible political and messianic implications. Perhaps they call to mind the passage from Zechariah 9:9 that Matthew later considers fulfilled in this triumphal entry. "Tell the daughter of Zion, Behold, your king is coming to you, humble, and mounted on an ass, and on a colt, the foal of an ass" (Matt. 21:5). These Pharisees insist that Jesus rebuke the crowd and so distance himself from this uninhibited outpouring of acclaim. Jesus replies, "I tell you, if these were silent, the very stones would cry out" (Luke 19:40). The report of these electric and disturbing events precedes Jesus to Jerusalem.

Jesus enters Jerusalem in the company of the joyful pilgrims and makes his way to the temple. According to the Gospel of John, Jesus previously had made a number of trips to Jerusalem and had visited and taught in the courts of the temple (John 7:14; 8:20; 10:23). He surveys the familiar scene of the beautiful temple complex and, as it has grown late, returns to Bethany for the night.

The next morning Jesus walks back to Jerusalem. Sunrise over Jerusalem from the Mount of Olives is an enchanting and unforgettable vision. The soft first rays of morning touch the hills beyond the city and then bathe in a warm glow the citadel, Herod the Great's splendid palace built along the city's western wall. The light grows brighter as it accelerates eastward across the Holy City, defining ever more sharply houses, buildings, and the temple. Jerusalem built of stones tinged golden is flooded with the light of a new day.

When Jesus arrives at the temple, pilgrims already crowd the temple complex. Herod the Great had built a series of courts leading to the sanctuary.[1] The spacious outer Court of the Gentiles is surrounded by beautiful

Jerusalem at sunrise.

colonnades and paved with large smooth stones. Here all races and nationalities are free to enter. Jews, both men and women, pass through a gate and come to the Court of the Women. A stone from this gate, recovered by archaeologists in 1935, warns in Greek and Latin that any Gentile entering beyond this gate will be subject to death.

On the west side of the Court of the Women fifteen semicircular steps lead up to the Nicanor Gate. Only Jewish men are allowed to enter this gate opening into the Court of Israel, a long narrow paved area from which one could look into the Court of the Priests. There on the great high altar, built of uncut stones, burns the sacrificial fire. The marvelous sanctuary faces east, reflecting the rays of the morning sun from walls covered with gold. Within the temple, the Holy of Holies is believed to enshrine the presence of God. Only the high priest could enter the Holy of

Holies on the Day of Atonement to atone with sacrificial blood for the sins of the people.

Daily sacrifices begin at dawn and last until late afternoon. During each day of passover week two bulls, a ram, a goat, and seven lambs are sacrificed.[2] Many private sacrifices are also offered, by which the worshiper seeks to gain and sustain a right relationship with God. Carefully trained priests perform each sacrificial rite according to ancient sacral traditions. At major feasts as many as 17,000 priests and Levites serve their two-week course at the temple, attending to the many tasks assigned them. At the top of this elaborate hierarchy overseeing all the various cultic functions is the high priest, assisted by 200 chief priests.

A sense of mystery and holiness overshadows the entire cultus. The worshiper witnessing the slaying of his sacrifice, the splashing of its blood on the great high altar, the smoke billowing toward heaven feels a deep sense of awe. He returns from the observance with the profound feeling of having drawn near to God and having expiated God's anger and displeasure for sins. The priests who regulate the functions at the temple, standing between the worshiper and God mediating the processes of thanksgiving and atonement, exercise powerful control over the people. As a rule the chief priests profit greatly from their privileged position and become aristocratic, wealthy, and politically influential.

Priestly hierarchical authority comes to a head in the high priest, who is finally responsible for the temple worship and also presides over the Sanhedrin, the Jewish Council that sits in judgment on religious and legal matters. On Yom Kippur, the Day of Atonement, he alone presides over the awe-inspiring temple ritual. Such a somber ceremony requires meticulous preparations to insure that the high priest will be ritually pure. A week prior to the Day of Atonement the high priest leaves home and lives in a special room at the temple to purify himself and to rehearse the proceedings. In the event that he should become defiled, a backup or understudy prepares to step in and preside.

On the morning of the Day of Atonement the high priest confesses his own sins and sacrifices a young bull to atone for them and for the priests' sins as well. Then he reverently enters the temple sanctuary and cautiously makes his way into the dark chamber of the Holy of Holies, where God's presence is believed to dwell. Only on this day of the year can he enter this most sacred chamber. According to the ancient ritual he sprinkles the bull's blood to atone for the sins of the people of Israel. It is a fearful time for the crowd gathered to await the high priest's return. Relief and joy greet him when atonement has been successfully gained for yet another year.[3]

Members of the high priestly families resided at Sepphoris; they tended to gravitate to centers of economic and political power and influence. The archives at Sepphoris preserved registers of priestly genealogies.[4]

A revealing episode involving priests at Sepphoris occurred during the last years of Herod the Great's reign, during the time that Matthias served as high priest.[5] On the night before the Day of Atonement, Matthias dreamed that he had sexual intercourse with a woman. When he awoke, he realized that he was defiled and disqualified from officiating the next day at the temple. His cousin, Jose ben Illem, a priest from Sepphoris, substituted as high priest for the sacred atonement ceremony. Priests from Sepphoris had close family ties with the Jerusalem priestly establishment and jealously guarded and nurtured these influential connections. From rabbinic sources "it is apparent that in the period before 70 C.E. Sepphoris was one of the few priestly towns in Galilee."[6]

When Jesus enters the Court of the Gentiles, he is met by a scene of thriving commercialization surrounding the cultic worship. Pilgrims from far and near crowd the court, busily negotiating purchases of oxen, sheep, pigeons, and lambs to sacrifice for the passover feast.[7]

These paschal lambs, less than one year old, must be officially approved by the priests. The Tyrian silver shekel is the only coinage acceptable for transactions at the temple, so pilgrims must convert their foreign money.[8] Bankers sit at special tables to change the foreign money for a substantial fee, indifferent to the complaints of their clients. The court reverberates with the noise of animals and the din of people haggling over the inflated prices of the sacrificial animals. "Back home," an irate pilgrim shouts, "a lamb this size would sell for half that price!" "Go home and buy it" is the merchant's caustic reply.

Jesus surveys the trafficking in the Court of the Gentiles, the only area at the temple where non-Jews are free to enter and pray (Mark 11:15–19). He makes a whip of cords (John 2:15) and drives out the merchants along with their animals. He turns over the money-changers' tables and, as the coins ring on the stone pavement, he recites brief passages from two of the great Hebrew prophets: "My house shall be called a house of prayer for all the nations" (Isa. 56:7). "But you have made it a den of robbers" (Jer. 7:11).

Jesus' radical assault on the commercialization of temple worship and the calloused disregard for the Gentiles' place of prayer come immediately to the attention of the chief priests and scribes. They determine to destroy Jesus, for such a disruption of the business of cultic observances cannot be tolerated. Neither can they endure the loss of the enormous profits derived from the temple sacrifices. Because of Jesus' widespread popularity they decide to proceed cautiously and first discredit him in the eyes of the people. They do not wish to appear to be killing a true prophet (Mark 11:18).[9]

Jesus departs from Jerusalem and stays overnight in Bethany. The next day, however, he appears again in the temple, where the chief priests, scribes, and elders are waiting for him. They ask him the first of several questions calculated to undermine his influence with the people and to provide a charge against him. "By what authority," they inquire, "are you doing these things, or who gave you this authority to do them?" (Mark 11:28). Jesus responds by saying that they must first answer his question before he answers theirs. "Was the baptism of John from heaven or from men? Answer me." His antagonists huddle and reason together. "If we say, 'From heaven,' he will say, 'Why did you not believe him?' But if we say, 'From men?' all the people will stone us; for they are convinced that John was a prophet" (Luke 20:5–6). They refuse to take either horn of the dilemma and reply, "We do not know." Then Jesus says, "Neither will I tell you by what authority I do these things."

The religious leaders continue their attempts to entrap Jesus, for it is becoming increasingly apparent that he threatens both their authority and institutions (Mark 12:12; Luke 20:19). "Is it lawful to pay taxes to Caesar, or not?" they ask. "Render to Caesar the things that are Caesar's," Jesus answers, "and to God the things that are God's" (Mark 12:17).

Then the Sadducees, the priestly party, pose a theoretical problem concerning a woman who had married sequentially seven brothers. Each husband had died leaving the woman childless. "In the resurrection whose wife will she be?" they ask. The Pharisees believe in the resurrection but the Sadducees do not. Jesus answers that in the resurrection there will not be marriages but people "are like angels in heaven" (Mark 12:25).

A scribe approaches and asks a standard question relative to the law. "Which commandment is the first of all?" Jesus begins by reciting the Shema from Deuteronomy 6:4: "'Hear, O Israel: The Lord our God, the Lord is one; and you shall love the Lord your God with all your heart, and with all your soul, and with all your mind, and with all your strength.' The second is this, 'You shall love your neighbor as yourself'" (Mark 12:29–31).

Tensions mount between Jesus and Jerusalem's religious hierarchy. Jesus' parables, some containing implicit criticisms of the chief priests, delight his audience but infuriate the Jewish leaders. Sharper words are exchanged and the chief priests and scribes can no longer tolerate Jesus' demands for reforms and renew their resolve to do away with him. They only must decide on the time and place out of public view, because they fear a riot by Jesus' followers (Mark 14:1–2).

Judas Iscariot, one of the twelve, conspires with the chief priests to betray Jesus into their hands for thirty pieces of silver, the traditional price of a slave. Judas' motive, the concern of much present-day speculation, is never stated.

Jesus' teachings assume an ominous air as he envisions the destruction of the Holy City and predicts that the temple, constructed of huge and beautiful Herodian ashlars, will be razed (Mark 13:1–4). These somber predictions of earthly tribulations interact with the apocalyptic vision of the parousia, when the Son of man will arrive on the clouds of glory with unspeakable power to judge all nations. In view of these coming cataclysmic events, Jesus' disciples must be prepared, watchful and radically loyal to God's sovereignty.

At the last supper, Jesus shares a passover meal or *seder* with his twelve apostles. The scene is a tranquil one in a large private upper room in Jerusalem, as they remember God's deliverance of his people from Egyptian bondage. The Gospel of John uses this setting for a lengthy discourse, Jesus' last will and testament, to his closest friends. The focus of the discourse is the statement, "This is my commandment, that you love one another as I have loved you. Greater love has no man than this, that a man lay down his life for his friends. You are my friends if you do what I command you" (John 15:12–14).

Jesus grows pensive. "But behold the hand of him who betrays me is with me on the table" (Luke 22:21). Each in turn asks, "Is it I, Lord?" (Matt. 26:22; Mark 14:19). Jesus equivocates. "It is one of the twelve, one who is dipping bread in the same dish with me. For the Son of man goes as it is written of him, but woe to that man by whom the Son of man is betrayed! It would have been better for that man if he had not been born" (Mark 14:20–21). The Gospel of John adds that Jesus dips a morsel and gives it to Judas, who soon excuses himself and goes out into the night (John 13:21–30).

Then Jesus turns and looks directly at Simon Peter. "Simon, Simon, behold Satan demanded to have you, that he might sift you like wheat, but I have prayed for you that your faith may not fail." Peter protests, "Lord, I am ready to go with you to prison and to death." Jesus' gives the memorable response, "I tell you, Peter, the cock will not crow this day, until you three times deny that you know me" (Luke 22:31–34).

While they are eating Jesus takes a piece of bread, blesses it, breaks it, and gives it to the apostles saying, "Take; this is my body." He lifts a cup of wine and gives thanks and hands it to them with the words, "This is my blood of the covenant, which is poured out for many. Truly, I say to you, I shall not drink again of the fruit of the vine until that day when I drink it new in the kingdom of God" (Matt. 26:26–29; Mark 14:22–25). Together they sing a familiar hymn and leave the upper room.

The apostles follow Jesus through the dimly lit streets of Jerusalem, out the eastern gate, down and across the brook Kidron and up the Mount of Olives. Here in a quiet garden, Gethsemane, where an olive press stands idle, one can look across to the monumental Herodian wall of the Holy City.

Jesus tells his apostles to sit in the garden while he goes to pray. But, he takes Peter, James, and John—often called "the inner circle" of the apostles—and reveals to them his inner turmoil. "My soul is very sorrowful," he begins, "even to death; remain here, and watch" (Mark 14:34). Proceeding a few paces, Jesus falls to the ground and prays, "Abba, Father, all things are possible to thee;

Olive tree in Gethsemane.

remove this cup from me; yet not what I will, but what thou wilt" (Mark 14:36). Returning to the apostles, who might have given support at this time of crisis, Jesus finds them asleep, unaware of the impending danger. "Watch and pray that you may not enter into temptation," Jesus admonishes them, "the spirit indeed is willing, but the flesh is weak" (Mark 14:38). He returns and prays a second and third time while the apostles continue to sleep.

From the Garden of Gethsemane Jesus can see the torches carried by the band of armed soldiers led by Judas from Jerusalem across Kidron and up the Mount of Olives. He could have fled into the darkness over the mount to Bethany or escaped into the desolate Judean hills. Jesus stands his ground as Judas comes to him and betrays him with a kiss—a prearranged signal for the temple guards. Startled from slumber Peter draws his sword and cuts off the ear of a slave of the high priest, Caiaphas. With this single blow, Peter puts his own life on the line by defending Jesus. But, Jesus steps in and rebukes Peter's violence. "Put your sword back into its place; for all who take the sword will perish by the sword" (Matt. 26:52). The "captains of the temple" seize Jesus and take him to Caiaphas.

The chief priests, scribes, and elders assemble to determine the charge to be brought against Jesus. The residence of Caiaphas, the high priest, must have been one of several great houses in the Upper City. Nahman Avigad's recent excavations in the Jewish Quarter of Jerusalem have unearthed a palatial mansion just south of the new stairs leading down to the Western Wall Plaza. This opulent residence, incorporating 6,500 square feet, had numerous rooms built around a large central court. The mansion, contemporary with Jesus' time, was burned in the destruction of Jerusalem in A.D. 70.[10] One room of special interest is a large hall measuring thirty-six feet by slightly over twenty-one feet. This beautifully decorated hall was ample enough to accommodate more than one hundred people.[11] Avigad cannot resist posing the intriguing prospect, "Might this have been the home of one of the High Priests, who were known to have lived in this quarter?"[12]

While the assembled members of the Jewish council, the Sanhedrin, interview those willing to testify against Jesus, Peter sits in the central courtyard warming himself by a fire kindled by some temple guards. A maid stares at Peter in the flickering light and says accusingly to the guards, "This man also was with him." Peter responds, "Woman, I do not know him" (Luke 22:56–57). Soon another person identifies Peter as "one of them." Again Peter denies. A third recognizes that Peter is from Galilee; the dialect of Galileans was offensive to Jerusalem Jews. "Certainly this man also was with him; for he is a Galilean." To this last challenge Peter fearfully blurts out, "Man, I do not know what you are saying." As Peter is speaking "the shrill clarion of the morn" crows and Peter, remembering the words of Jesus, breaks down and goes out shedding bitter tears (Luke 22: 59–62).

At dawn the chief priests and the entire council begin to hear witnesses testify against Jesus. Their testimony, frequently contradictory and even false, proves insufficient to warrant a death penalty. The key witness for the prosecution is Jesus himself. When asked directly, "Are you the Christ, the Son of the Blessed?" he answers, "I am; and you will see the Son of man sitting at the right hand of Power, and coming with the clouds of heaven" (Mark 14:61–62). Hearing this confession, the high priest tears his robe and says to the Sanhedrin, "Why do we still need witnesses? You have heard his blasphemy. What is your decision?" "Death!" they respond.

The Jewish authorities send Jesus bound to Pontius Pilate, the Roman prefect or governor, who had come up from his official residence in Caesarea Maritima to be in Jerusalem during passover. Pilate had been appointed to this important frontier post by the emperor Tiberius. The authorities charge Jesus with perverting the Jewish nation and forbidding the Jews to pay tribute to Caesar. Then they add that Jesus claims to be Christ a king. Pilate, as they well knew, could not turn a deaf ear to such accusations of treason. Pilate looks at Jesus, a Galilean rabbi in his bonds, and asks matter of factly, "Are you the King of the Jews?" "You have said so," Jesus replies and then remains silent (Mark 15:1–5).

The Sanhedrin.

Pilate, aware that Jesus is a Galilean, is informed that Herod Antipas, tetrarch of Galilee and Peraea, has arrived in Jerusalem to celebrate the feast of passover. Antipas has come from his royal residence in Sepphoris or Tiberias. Pilate may know that Antipas had attempted unsuccessfully to arrest and interrogate Jesus. As a good will gesture and to learn more about Jesus' activities in Galilee, Pilate sends him to Antipas, who is pleased to meet Jesus and hopes to see him perform some sign. Jesus is still silent before Antipas' questions and the impassioned accusations of the chief priests and scribes. So Antipas and his soldiers contemptuously mock Jesus, dress him in a gorgeous robe, and return him to Pilate. Luke observes that Pilate and Antipas had been enemies but after this episode became friends. One can hardly fail to see the irony in the meeting between Jesus and Antipas, who had lived very near one another for three decades. Finally they meet but remain far apart (Luke 23:6–16).

Pilate summons the authorities, whom he realizes are envious of Jesus' popularity, and suggests that he release Jesus, "the king of the Jews." But, the crowd, gathered and orchestrated by the chief priests, cries out for the release of Barabbas, imprisoned for murder and insurrection. "Then what shall I do with the man whom you call the King of the Jews?" Pilate asks. "Crucify him! Crucify him!" the crowd chants (Mark 15:6–14). "If you release this man, you are not Caesar's friend; every one who makes himself a king sets himself against Caesar" (John 19:12).

Soon after Pilate's arrival in Judea in A.D. 26 he learned how uncompromising these religious authorities could be. Now he is unwilling to deny them Jesus, although their charges against him are questionable. Josephus recounts that not long after Pilate came to Judea, he and some of his troops traveled from his governor's palace in Caesarea to Jerusalem.[13] They entered the city after dark and set up the Roman military standards, symbols of Roman authority bearing the emperor Tiberius' image. This was a customary practice. Pilate, however, was ignorant of the Jews' law forbidding idolatry and that previous governors had honored the Jews' proscription of idols. (These governors had brought Roman standards into Jerusalem that did not bear the emperor's image.)

The next morning when the Jews discovered the emperor's images, they were outraged, but Pilate had already returned to Caesarea. A large delegation of officials and others from Jerusalem followed Pilate to Caesarea to entreat him to remove the images. Pilate felt that should he remove them it would be interpreted as an affront to imperial power and prestige. After letting the Jews wait for six days, Pilate granted them a hearing in the great stadium that Herod the Great had built. Pilate gave orders that his soldiers secretly surround the stadium as soon as the Jews were inside. Then he mounted the podium to hear their petition. As the Jews were pleading their case, Pilate gave a prearranged signal and the soldiers surrounded the supplicants, prepared to kill any who resisted. The defenseless Jews fell to the ground and bared their necks to the Roman swords, stating that they much preferred death to violating God's sacred law.

Caught by surprise at this unexpected demonstration of unyielding religious fervor, Pilate relented and ordered that the standards bearing the emperor's image be retrieved from Jerusalem. How could this newly appointed prefect justify to the emperor the slaughter of so many of Jerusalem's unarmed religious leaders? This was a lesson on intimidation and manipulation remembered by both Pilate and the Jewish officials.

Pilate attempts to pacify the Jewish authorities and the people by consenting to Jesus' crucifixion but first he has his soldiers scourge Jesus. The Roman scourge (*flagrum*) had been sadistically designed to inflict excruciating pain. It was a leather whip to which sharp pieces of bone and metal were attached. The lash cut and tore away the flesh causing profuse bleeding. Some criminals condemned to be crucified did not survive the scourge.

Pilate's soldiers take Jesus into the "palace," traditionally identified as the huge fortress of Antonia, just north of the temple complex. Herod the Great erected the Antonia shortly after capturing Jerusalem in 37 B.C. and named it in honor of his patron Mark Antony. Within its massive walls was a great paved court, from which stones have been excavated beneath the convent of the Sisters of Zion. In this court the entire battalion, between four and six hundred soldiers, assembles to mock and ridicule Jesus.[14] Dressed in a robe of royal purple with a crown plaited of thorns pressed down on his head, Jesus endures the calloused taunts of the raucous soldiers. They hit him on the head with a reed, spit on him, and jeer at him. "Hail, king of the Jews!" Having played out their mock show of regal power, the soldiers dress Jesus in his own clothes and lead him toward Golgotha, the place of a skull, and crucifixion.

Jesus bears his cross[15] through the streets of Jerusalem followed by a large crowd in which women weep unrestrained. He turns to them and says, "Daughters of Jerusalem, do not weep for me, but weep for yourselves and for your children" (Luke 23:28). This way of sorrow, commemorated today by the Via Dolorosa, leads outside the city wall to the place for public executions. Along the way a pilgrim, Simon of Cyrene from north Africa, is compelled to carry the cross to Golgotha. When they arrive, Jesus is offered a drink of wine laced with myrrh to ease the pain. But he refuses it. "There they crucified him" (Luke 23:33), nailing his hands and feet to the cross and lifting it upright. The writer of the Gospel of John later will see in this lifting up an ironic form of exaltation, where the power of self-giving love is most dramatically revealed. Jesus had predicted, "I, when I am lifted up from the earth, will draw all men to myself" (John 12:32).

The sign (*titulus*) that Pilate has ordered placed above Jesus' head states in Hebrew, Latin, and Greek for all to read, "The King of the Jews."

Public crucifixion, a horrible way to die, was excruciating and slow, calculated to deter future criminals.[16] The Romans perfected this ancient form of execution. Thousands upon thousands of Jews were crucified during this period and when Jerusalem fell to the Romans in A.D. 70. Of the many Jews crucified, Josephus notes the death of Jesus in a paragraph that has obviously been retouched by a pious Christian hand:

> About this time there lived Jesus, a wise man, if indeed one ought to call him a man. For he was one who wrought surprising feats and was a teacher of such people as accept the truth gladly. He won over many Jews and many of the Greeks. He was the Messiah. When Pilate, upon hearing him accused by men of the highest standing amongst us, had condemned him to be crucified, those who had in the first place come to love him did not give up their affection for him. On the third day he appeared to them restored to life, for the prophets of God had prophesied these and countless other marvellous things about him. And the tribe of Christians, so called after him, has still to this day not disappeared.[17]

The Gospels choose not to detail the agony of Jesus but his words from the cross are indelibly etched in the memory of the Christian community. Looking down upon those responsible for his crucifixion he prays,

Roman military standard.

205

"Father, forgive them; for they know not what they do" (Luke 23:34). To one of the two criminals crucified on either side Jesus gives the promise, "Truly, I say to you, today you will be with me in Paradise" (Luke 23:43). Seeing Mary and the Beloved Disciple near the foot of the cross, Jesus thinks of his mother and says to her, "Woman, behold, your son!" and to him, "Behold, your mother!" (John 19:26–27). Parched with thirst from dehydration and loss of blood, Jesus acknowledges his human frailty: "I thirst" (John 19:28). Overshadowed by the terrible loneliness of approaching death, he echoes in Aramaic the opening lines of Psalm 22, *"Eloi, Eloi, lama sabachthani?"* "My God, my God, why hast thou forsaken me?" (Mark 15:34; cf. Matt. 27:46). Finally, he cries out, "Father, into thy hands I commit my spirit" (Luke 23:46) and gasps, "It is finished" (John 19:30).

A centurion facing Jesus says, "Truly, this was the Son of God!" (Matt. 27:54; Mark 15:39). A soldier pierces his side with a spear (John 19:34). Joseph of Arimathea, an influential member of the Sanhedrin who had not consented to Jesus' death, obtains Pilate's permission to bury Jesus' body. Joseph takes the body down, wraps it in a linen shroud, and places it in a rock-hewn tomb that had never been used. Confused and broken-hearted, his disciples go their own ways. To the disinterested casual observer the matter of Jesus' revival movement appears to be laid to rest.

But the power of Jesus' life lives in the community of faith that exalts him as Savior. His disciples tell of discovering the tomb empty and of various encounters with the risen Lord. Their faith in the resurrection is a historical fact that has significantly directed and shaped Western culture. His followers carry forth the challenge that Jesus had proclaimed by the sea and in the city—to accept the kingdom of God and live in the knowledge that a merciful God is sovereign over all his creation.[18]

Conclusion

Hello, Strange speaking," the voice over the phone answered. "Jim," I responded, "I am ready to write the conclusion to the book on Jesus and the city. What do you think is the significance of the excavations at Sepphoris?" It was more than a decade earlier that Jim, Carolyn, and I had made our first walking tour of Sepphoris, although we previously had visited the site separately. There was a brief silence while I held the receiver in anticipation. Then came Jim's clear and crisp assessment, "It is there!" This seemed so obvious at first I thought he was joking. Then I realized this indeed is where we must begin. "It is there," I repeated silently. We had rediscovered a forgotten city. Thousands upon thousands of pieces of datable pottery, a dozen colors of imported marble, fragments of bright frescos, artistically molded plaster, smooth, round, limestone columns, ornately cut capitals, hundreds of coins, scores of whole ceramic vessels, beautiful mosiacs, bronze figures, gold chain, carved ivory, and other artifacts all demonstrate that Sepphoris, in the early and middle Roman periods, was indeed a thriving metropolis.

Josephus accurately reported that after the destruction of Sepphoris in 4 B.C., Antipas rebuilt the city on the grand model of a splendid Roman capital. The seat of government, Sepphoris boasted Antipas' opulent royal residence, the necessary administrative offices, the royal bank, and archives. Government officials and courtiers busily tended to the king's affairs. Within the city's strongly fortified walls stood the great fortress, headquarters for Antipas' secret police and the military personnel charged with keeping the peace and protecting the borders.

Sepphoris' economic wealth derived in large measure from the rich deep soil of the Bet Netofa Valley north of the city. This large area of fertile land, combined with ample annual rainfall, produced an abundant supply of food for the city's growing population soon reaching thirty thousand. Crops and rental income from Antipas' personal estate in the valley provided a basic source of his considerable wealth. Sepphoris guarded major trade routes that intersected in the valley. These highways linked Sepphoris commercially with ports on the Mediterranean—Caesarea Maritima, Ptolemais (Akko), Tyre, and Sidon—as well as Jerusalem, the Greek cities of Decapolis, Antioch, Damascus, and Petra. Taxes collected from merchants and other travelers through Galilee provided lucrative revenues.

During the centuries following the conquest of Alexander the Great, the people living in Galilee were caught up in cross-currents of traditional Judaism and Greek and Roman cultures. New and attractive ideas and forces challenged old values and assumptions about the meaning of life and the nature of God. To these people, Jesus proclaimed the good news of the kingdom of God, responded to their questions, and addressed their burning issues. The Gospels portrayed Jesus as skillfully drawing on images from their shared experiences in Galilee—not only pastoral scenes with shepherds and sowers but also urban images with kings, merchants, tax collectors, and dramatic actors.

The urbanization of Galilee points to the probability that Jesus spoke Greek as well as Aramaic. Present-day debates among New Testament scholars are turning from the question of whether Jesus spoke Greek to how well he spoke Greek. Careful study of the Greek text of the Gospels has led to the conclusion that Jesus delivered a number of parables originally in Greek rather than Aramaic. The sayings of Jesus contained in the Gospels, therefore, may be closer to the actual words of Jesus than previously thought.

The realization that Jesus grew up in the shadow of Sepphoris, a burgeoning Roman capital city, casts new light on the man and his message—light that changes the perception of Jesus as a rustic from the remote hills of Galilee. The people to whom Jesus proclaimed his message of hope and salvation, whether Jews, Greeks, Romans, or other Gentiles, were struggling with life's meaning in a culture where Jewish traditions and Greco-Roman urban values collided. Jesus' teachings reflect a shared awareness of city life with his cosmopolitan audience.

Following the crucifixion, the message of Jesus came to focus on Jesus himself as the messiah and revealer of the kingdom of God. The movement he founded was from the beginning prepared to address and meet the religious concerns of many lost in the vast Roman Empire. His message of hope and love gained ready acceptance throughout the major cities of the Roman world. A quarter-century after Jesus' death, Paul wrote to Christians in the Eternal City, "your faith is proclaimed in all the world" (Rom. 1:8). As the Roman Empire fell into decline, the Christians' proclamation of salvation provided hope and direction for renewed life in the great metropolitan centers—a message with meaning for life in the city and the promise of a better world.

Notes

Introduction

1. Leroy Waterman, *Preliminary Report of the University of Michigan Excavations at Sepphoris, Palestine, in 1931* (Ann Arbor: University of Michigan Press, 1937), p. v. The name "Sepphoris" means "bird" because (according to a postbiblical source) it is perched on a hill like a bird. See pp. 18, 26.

2. The report on this project can be found in Richard A. Batey, "Subsurface Interface Radar at Sepphoris, Israel, 1985," *Journal of Field Archaeology* 14 (Spring 1987): 1–8.

3. *The Innocents Abroad* (New York: P. F. Collier & Son, 1869), 2:245.

Chapter 1

1. Josephus, *Jewish Antiquities* 15.361. Classical sources cited from the Loeb Classical Library.

2. Josephus, *Jewish War* 1.277.

3. Ibid., 1.271–72, 278.

4. Ibid., 1.279.

5. Ibid., 1.280–85.

6. *Jewish Antiquities* 13.338–43. Pottery sherds found at Sepphoris date to Iron Age II (1000–900 B.C.). See James F. Strange, "Sepphoris," a forthcoming article in the *Anchor Bible Dictionary*.

7. *Jewish War* 1.170.

8. Ibid., 1.304.

9. Michael Grant, *Herod the Great* (New York: American Heritage, 1971), p. 75.

10. *Jewish War* 1.361–63.

11. Dio Cassius, *Roman History* 50.35; cf. Plutarch, *Antony* 65.1; 66.5.

12. *Jewish War* 1.386–92; *Jewish Antiquities* 15.187–96.

13. *Jewish War* 1.394–96; *Jewish Antiquities* 15.199–201.

14. Grant, *Herod the Great*, p. 128.

15. *Jewish Antiquities* 15.271.

16. Ibid., 15.268–70.

17. Ibid., 15.273.

18. Ibid., 15.272f.

19. Ibid., 15.271.

20. Ibid., 15.275–80.

21. Ibid., 15.284–91.

22. Grant, *Herod the Great*, p. 127.

23. Ibid., pp. 163f.

24. *Jewish Antiquities* 16.14f.; Grant, *Herod the Great*, p. 176.

25. Robert L. Hohlfelder, "Herod the Great's City on the Sea," *National Geographic* 171 (February 1987): 277; *Jewish War* 1.407–15.

26. Hohlfelder, "City on the Sea," p. 262.

27. *Jewish Antiquities* 16.16–26.

28. *Jewish War* 1.659f., 665.

29. Ibid. 1.670–73.

30. Harold W. Hoehner, *Herod Antipas* (Cambridge: Cambridge University Press, 1972; reprint, Grand Rapids: Zondervan, 1980), p. 31; *Jewish Antiquities* 17.188; *Jewish War* 1.668.

31. Hoehner, *Herod Antipas*, p. 39.

32. Seán Freyne, *Galilee from Alexander the Great to Hadrian 323 B.C.E. to 135 C.E.* (Wilmington: Michael Glazier, 1980), p. 123; *Jewish War* 2.56; *Jewish Antiquities* 17.271f.

33. *Life* 232.

34. *Jewish Antiquities* 18.27; Eric M. Meyers, Ehud Netzer, and Carol Meyers, "Sepphoris 'Ornament of All Galilee,'" *Biblical Archaeologist* 49 (March 1986):8. A coin minted at Sepphoris during the reign of the emperor Caracalla displays a temple.

35. Hoehner, *Herod Antipas*, p. 15; *Jewish Antiquities* 15.342f.

36. Leonardo B. Dal Maso, *Rome of the Caesars* (Firenze: Bonechi-Edizioni "Il Turismo," 1974), pp. 27f.

37. Ibid., pp. 26f.

38. Ibid., p. 27.

39. Ibid., pp. 56–61.

40. Ernest Nash, *Pictorial Dictionary of Ancient Rome* (New York: Praeger, 1961), 1:63.

41. Maso, *Rome of the Caesars*, pp. 102f.

42. Margarete Bieber, *The History of the Greek and Roman Theater* (Princeton: Princeton University Press, 1939), p. 349; Suetonius, "The Deified Augustus," *Lives of the Caesars* 2:43.

43. Maso, *Rome of the Caesars*, pp. 81–85.

44. Ibid., p. 10f.; Will Durant, *Caesar and Christ* (New York: Simon & Schuster, 1944), pp. 233–58.

45. Hoehner, *Herod Antipas*, pp. 31–33.

Chapter 2

1. Richard A. Batey, "'Is Not This the Carpenter?'" *New Testament Studies* 30 (April 1984): 249, 256 n. 1; Douglas E. Oakman, *Jesus and the Economic Questions of His Day* (Lewiston: Edwin Mellen, 1986), pp. 176–82.

2. Kaari Ward, ed., *Jesus and His Times* (Pleasantville: Reader's Digest , 1987), pp. 63f., 111f. See also J. Robert Teringo, *The Land and People Jesus Knew* (Minneapolis: Bethany House, 1985), pp. 108–13.

3. See Paul Hanly Furfey, "Christ as Tekton," *Catholic Bible Quarterly* 17 (April 1955): 215; Samuel Krauss, *Talmudische Archeologie* (Leipzig: G. Fock, 1910–12; reprint, Hildesheim: Georg Olms, 1966), 2:266–69.

4. *Jesus, A New Biography* (Chicago: University of Chicago Press, 1927), pp. 205f.; and "Jesus and Sepphoris," *Journal of Biblical Literature* 45 (1926): 18.

5. Virgil, *Aeneid* 1.420–33.

6. Batey, "Carpenter?" p. 257 n. 2.

7. See William L. MacDonald, *The Architecture of the Roman Empire*, vol. 2 (New Haven and London: Yale University Press, 1986).

8. J. G. Landels, *Engineering in the Ancient World* (Los Angeles: University of California Press, 1978), pp. 63–67; James F. Strange, "Sepphoris," forthcoming article in the *Anchor Bible Dictionary*.

9. Landels, *Engineering in the Ancient World*, pp. 84–98.

10. Roy William Davis, "The Daily Life of a Roman Soldier the Principate," *Aufstieg und Niedergang der Romischen Welt* (New York: Walter de Gruyter, 1974), 2:329f.

11. Louise Gardner, *Art Through the Ages*, 6th ed. (New York: Harcourt Brace Jovanovich, 1926, 1975), pp. 222–25; Spiro Kostof, *A History of Architecture* (New York: Oxford University Press, 1985), p. 195; John Julius Norwich, ed., *Great Architecture of the World* (New York: Random House, 1975), p. 76; Frank Sear, *Roman Architecture* (New York: Cornell University Press, 1982), pp. 66f., 78f.

12. Landels, *Engineering in the Ancient World*, p. 65.

Chapter 3

1. Richard A. Batey, "Jesus and the Theatre," *New Testament Studies* 30 (October 1984): 563f.; Ulrich Wilckens, *Theological Dictionary of the New Testament*, ed. G. W. Bromiley (Grand Rapids: Eerdmans, 1972), 8:567f.

2. F. V. Filson, *A Commentary on the Gospel According to St. Matthew* (New York: Harper & Brothers, 1960), p. 93. See also Alexander Jones, *The Gospel According to St. Matthew* (New York: Sheed & Ward, 1965), p. 85; David Hill, *The Gospel of Matthew* (London: Marshall, Morgan & Scott, 1972), p. 133; Jack P. Lewis, *The Gospel According to Matthew* (Austin, Tex.: Sweet, 1976), 1:99.

3. J. P. Meier, *Matthew* (Wilmington: Michael Glazier, 1980), p. 58. "The classical meaning of the Greek word is 'actor in a play.' The corresponding Aramaic word means 'a profane person.' A second-century rabbi remarked acidly that 'there are ten portions of hypocrisy in the world, and nine of them are in Jerusalem'" (Sherman E. Johnson, "The Gospel According to Matthew," *The Interpreter's Bible* [New York: Abingdon, 1951], 7:306).

4. James F. Strange pointed out to me that the Greek word translated as "street corners" (*plateiōn*) is the plural of *plateia* or colonnaded street. The main street of Sepphoris is referred to as *palatia* in rabbinic sources (Berakhoth 3; Y Ketub. 1.10). Strange translates: "And when you pray, you must not be like actors, for they love to stand and pray in [public] assemblies and on the corners of the [colonnaded] streets to be seen by people." Strange stated this idea in an unpublished paper read at the annual meeting of the Society of Biblical Literature, November 20, 1988.

5. Lewis, *Matthew*, 1:98f. R. Halafta, a first-century rabbi, made it a religious custom at Sepphoris, the residence of influential priestly families, to sound a ram's horn or a trumpet following benedictions (*Babylonian Talmud*, Rosh Hashanah 27a and Taanith 16b).

6. *The Prophet* (New York: Alfred A. Knopf, 1965), pp. 19f.

7. Margarete Bieber, *The History of the Greek and Roman Theater* (Princeton: Princeton University Press, 1961), p. 161.

8. Leroy Waterman, *Preliminary Report of the University of Michigan Excavations at Sepphoris, Palestine, in 1931* (Ann Arbor: University of Michigan Press, 1937), p. 29: "That the theater was in existence in the reign of Herod Antipas there can scarcely be a doubt. . . . Two things emerge as very certain. First, it is scarcely possible under the circumstances to place the theater later than Herod Antipas. Second, it is equally impossible to think of locating it earlier than Herod the Great, since no Hasmonean Jew could be conceived of as builder of a theater."

9. James F. Strange and Thomas R. W. Longstaff, "Sepphoris (Sippori), 1986 (II)," *Israel Exploration Journal* 37 (1987): 280; see also Strange's forthcoming article on Sepphoris in the *Anchor Bible Dictionary*; Eric M. Meyers, Ehud Netzer, and Carol Meyers, "Sepphoris, 'Ornament of All Galilee,'" *Biblical Archaeologist* 49 (March 1986): 13; Eric Meyers, Ehud Netzer, and Carol Meyers, "Sepphoris (Sippori), 1986 (I)—Joint Sepphoris Project," *Israel Exploration Journal* 37 (1987): 278.

10. Bieber, *History of the Greek and Roman Theater*, p. 227; Suetonius, "The Deified Augustus," *The Lives of the Caesars* 2.43.1–5.

11. Suetonius, *Lives of the Caesars* 2.99.1.

12. Vitruvius, *On Architecture* 5.6.1.

13. Ibid., 5.6.3; Bieber, *History of the Greek and Roman Theater*, p. 187; J. T. Allen, *Stage Antiquities of the Greeks and Romans and Their Influences* (New York: Cooper Square, 1963), pp. 91–97.

14. Vitruvius, *On Architecture* 5.9.1.

15. Ibid., 5.6.8–9.

16. Bieber, *History of the Greek and Roman Theater*, pp. 179f.

17. Vitruvius, *On Architecture* 5.5.1–8.

18. Josephus, *Jewish Antiquities* 15.267–72.

19. M. Rostovtzeff, *The Social and Economic History of the Hellenistic World* (Oxford: Clarendon, 1941), 3:1048, 1085. See also Eric M. Meyers, Ehud Netzer, and Carol L. Meyers, "Artistry in Stone, The Mosaics of Ancient Sepphoris," *Biblical Archaeologist* 50 (December 1987): 223–31.

20. Meyer Reinhold, *Classical Drama, Greek and Roman* (New York: Barron's Educational Series, 1959), pp. 204–69.

21. Fragment 9, lines 7–9, from Carl R. Holladay, *Fragments from Hellenistic Jewish Authors: Poets* (Atlanta: Scholars, 1989), pp. 315, 371; Howard Jacobson, *The Exagoge of Ezekiel* (Cambridge: Cambridge University Press, 1983), p. 99.

22. Josephus, *Jewish Antiquities* 19.343–50.

Chapter 4

1. Harold W. Hoehner, *Herod Antipas* (Cambridge: Cambridge University Press, 1972; reprint, Grand Rapids: Zondervan, 1980), pp. 130f.

2. Herodias' father was Aristobulus, a son of Herod the Great and Mariamne I, Herod's Hasmonean wife. Herodias' mother was Berenice, the daughter of Herod the Great's sister, Salome, and her husband Costobarus. Herodias was born between 9 and 7 B.C. and would have been around thirty-seven years old when she married Antipas in approximately A.D. 29. See Hoehner, *Herod Antipas*, pp. 154f., 349.

3. The Mosaic law strictly forbade a man from marrying his living brother's wife (see Lev. 18:16; 20:21). A man was obligated, however, to marry the widow of his deceased brother and have a son who would perpetuate his dead brother's name (the levirate law; Deut. 25:5–10).

4. Josephus also gives an account of John's incarceration and death that supplements the Gospel record (*Jewish Antiquities* 18.116–19).

5. Hoehner, *Herod Antipas*, p. 130; Josephus, *Jewish Antiquities* 18.109.

6. Hoehner, *Herod Antipas*, pp. 142f.

7. Josephus, *Jewish Antiquities* 18.109f. Josephus gives the name of Antipas' half-brother (Herodias' first husband) as "Herod." The Gospels refer to him as "Philip" (Matt. 14:3; Mark 6:17; Luke 3:19). Either his name was Herod Philip—and so both Josephus and the Gospel writers are correct (Hoehner, *Herod Antipas*, p. 136)—or the Gospel writers have confused Herod with Philip the tetrarch. See Emil Schürer, *The History of the Jewish People in the Age of Jesus Christ (175 B.C.–A.D. 135)* (Edinburgh: T. & T. Clark, 1973), 1:344.

8. Josephus, *Jewish Antiquities* 18.110.

9. Ibid., 18.113.

10. Ibid., 17.119.

11. Hoehner, *Herod Antipas*, p. 145.

12. Josephus, *Jewish War* 7.171–77.

13. Ibid., 7.172, 186–89.

14. Josephus, *Jewish Antiquities* 18.118.

15. Ibid., 18.113. Josephus probably refers to Gabala, a district south of Moabitis in Idumaea.

16. Ibid., 18.115.

17. Ibid., 18.116–19.

18. Ibid., 18.237–38.

19. Ibid., 18.143–50; Schürer, *History*, pp. 443–45.

20. Josephus, *Jewish Antiquities* 18.168–69, 186–91.

21. Ibid., 18.224, 237.

22. Ibid., 18.240–46.

23. Ibid., 18.247–55.

Chapter 5

1. Joachim Jeremias, *The Parables of Jesus* (New York: Charles Scribner's Sons, 1963), p. 210.

2. Josephus, *Jewish Antiquities* 17.319.

3. Jack P. Lewis, *The Gospel According to Matthew* (Austin, Tex.: Sweet, 1976), 2:61.

4. John R. Donahue, *The Gospel in Parable* (Philadelphia: Fortress, 1988), p. 75.

5. Eta Linnemann, *Jesus of the Parables* (New York: Harper & Row, 1966), p. 110.

6. Pheme Perkins, *Hearing the Parables of Jesus* (New York: Paulist, 1981), p. 128.

7. Jeremias, *Parables of Jesus*, p. 58; C. H. Dodd, *The Parables of the Kingdom* (London: Nisbet, 1936), p. 147.

8. S. MacLean Gilmour, "The Gospel According to St. Luke," *The Interpreter's Bible*

(New York: Abingdon, 1952), 8:328; Perkins, *Hearing the Parables of Jesus*, pp. 146f.

9. Josephus, *Jewish War* 2.80–97, 111; *Jewish Antiquities* 17.299–302, 311–14, 318, 342–44.

10. Jeremias, *Parables of the Kingdom*, p. 59.

11. Dan O. Via, Jr., *The Parables* (Philadelphia: Fortress, 1967), p. 119.

12. Dodd, *Parables of the Kingdom*, pp. 152f.

13. Jeremias, *Parables of Jesus*, pp. 63–66.

14. Linnemann, *Jesus of the Parables*, p. 94.

15. Donahue, *Gospel in Parable*, p. 95.

16. Jeremias, *Parables of Jesus*, p. 64; Via, *Parables*, p. 129.

17. Gilmour, "St. Luke," p. 516.

18. Donahue, *Gospel in Parable*, p. 142; Dodd, *Parables of the Kingdom*, p. 114.

19. Josephus, *Jewish Antiquities* 18.252.

20. Lewis, *Matthew*, p. 50.

21. Ibid., p. 51.

22. Eric M. Meyers and James F. Strange, *Archaeology, the Rabbis, and Early Christianity* (Nashville: Abingdon, 1981), p. 60.

23. George A. Buttrick, *The Parables of Jesus* (New York: Harper, 1928), p. 7.

24. Gilmour, "St. Luke," p. 382.

25. Jeremias, *Parables of Jesus*, pp. 206–9.

26. Lewis, *Matthew*, p. 140.

27. Dodd, *Parables of the Kingdom*, pp. 85–88.

28. The image of king and God as King appear frequently in the Old Testament.

Chapter 6

1. Harold W. Hoehner, *Herod Antipas* (Cambridge: Cambridge University Press, 1972; reprint, Grand Rapids: Zondervan, 1980), pp. 70–73; Seán Freyne, *Galilee from Alexander the Great to Hadrian 323 B.C.E. to 135 C.E.* (Wilmington: Michael Glazier, 1980), pp. 165–67; A. N. Sherwin-White, *Roman Society and Roman Law in the New Testament* (London: Oxford University Press, 1963), p. 139; Douglas R. Edwards, "First Century Urban/ Rural Relations in Lower Galilee: Exploring the Archaeological and Literary Evidence," *Society of Biblical Literature 1988 Seminar Papers* (Atlanta: Scholars, 1988), pp. 172–79.

2. Josephus, *Jewish War* 3.42.

3. John H. Hayes, *Introduction to the Bible* (Philadelphia: Westminster, 1971), p. 37.

4. Hoehner, *Herod Antipas*, pp. 52, 291–95.

5. Josephus, *Life* 235.

6. Hayes, *Introduction to the Bible*, p. 42.

7. Ibid.

8. Kaari Ward, ed., *Jesus and His Times* (Pleasantville: Reader's Digest, 1987), pp. 42, 77.

9. Hoehner, *Herod Antipas*, pp. 67f.; Freyne, *Galilee from Alexander the Great*, pp. 173f.

10. Josephus, *Jewish War* 2.635.

11. Shelly Wachsmann, "The Galilee Boat—2,000-year-old Hull Recovered Intact," *Biblical Archaeology Review* 14 (September–October 1988): 19f.

12. Ibid., p. 27.

13. Ibid., p. 31.

14. Hoehner, *Herod Antipas*, p. 70; Freyne, *Galilee from Alexander the Great*, p. 165.

15. Seán Freyne, *Galilee, Jesus and the Gospels* (Philadelphia: Fortress, 1988), pp. 143–55; *Galilee from Alexander the Great*, p. 176.

16. Richard A. Batey, "Subsurface Interface Radar at Sepphoris, Israel, 1985," *Journal of Field Archaeology* 14 (Spring 1987): 6f.

17. Freyne, *Galilee from Alexander the Great*, p. 165; Sherwin-White, *Roman Society and Roman Law*, p. 140.

18. Josephus, *Jewish Antiquities* 18.261–304; Freyne, *Galilee, Jesus and the Gospels*, p. 159; *Galilee from Alexander the Great*, p. 166.

19. Josephus, *Jewish Antiquities* 18.300.

20. Freyne, *Galilee, Jesus and the Gospels*, pp. 94–96.

21. J. Andrew Overman, "Who Were the First Urban Christians? Urbanization in Galilee in the First Century," *Society of Biblical Literature 1988 Seminar Papers* (Atlanta: Scholars, 1988), p. 161.

Chapter 7

1. Richard Batey, *Jesus and the Poor* (New York: Harper & Row, 1972), p. 9.

2. Seán Freyne, *Galilee, Jesus and the Gospels* (Philadelphia: Fortress, 1988), pp. 74f.

3. Harold W. Hoehner, *Herod Antipas* (Cambridge: Cambridge University Press, 1972; reprint, Grand Rapids: Zondervan, 1980), p. 54; Günther Bornkamm, *Jesus of Nazareth* (New York: Harper, 1959), pp. 153f.

4. Gerd Theissen, *The First Followers of Jesus* (London: SCM, 1978), pp. 41–46.

5. Seán Freyne, *Galilee from Alexander the Great to Hadrian 323 B.C.E. to 135 C.E.* (Notre Dame: University of Notre Dame Press, 1980), pp. 127, 181f.

6. Batey, *Jesus and the Poor*, p. 20.

7. Bornkamm, *Jesus of Nazareth*, pp. 91–93: "Just as we do not ascribe to Jesus merely the preaching of a 'realized eschatology' (C. H. Dodd), we should not make him an apocalypticist who merely renews the old expectations of late Jewish hopes in a more vivid form, and ascribe in either case the other view to the church" (p. 91).

8. C. H. Dodd, *The Parables of the Kingdom* (London: Nisbet, 1935), pp. 53–56.

9. Bornkamm, *Jesus of Nazareth*, pp. 117–24.

10. Pheme Perkins, *Hearing the Parables of Jesus* (New York: Paulist, 1981), p. 71: "The rich man in the parable is rather typical of the picture of the rich in this preaching. 1 Enoch suggests that their lack of concern for Moses and the prophets was based on the prosperity and happiness of their earthly life."

11. Frederick C. Grant, "The Gospel According to St. Mark," *The Interpreter's Bible* (New York: Abingdon, 1951), 7:806f.

12. Theissen, *First Followers*, p. 11.

13. Joachim Jeremias, *The Parables of Jesus* (New York: Charles Scribner's Sons, 1963), pp. 214–16.

14. Sherman E. Johnson, "The Gospel According to St. Matthew," *The Interpreter's Bible* (New York: Abingdon, 1951), 7:323.

15. John R. Donahue, *The Gospel in Parable* (Philadelphia: Fortress, 1988), p. 211.

16. S. MacLean Gilmour, "The Gospel According to St. Luke," *The Interpreter's Bible* (New York: Abingdon, 1952), 8:239.

17. Eta Linnemann, *Jesus of the Parables* (New York: Harper & Row, 1966), pp. 53–56.

18. Donahue, *Gospel in Parable*, p. 129.

19. Halvor Moxnes, *The Economy of the Kingdom* (Philadelphia: Fortress, 1988), pp. 93–98.

20. Johnson, "St. Matthew," p. 422.

21. Perkins, *Hearing the Parables of Jesus*, pp. 134–37; Moxnes, *Economy of the Kingdom*, pp. 154–59.

22. Johnson, "St. Matthew," p. 340.

23. Jack P. Lewis, *The Gospel According to Matthew* (Austin, Tex.: Sweet, 1976), 1:122f.

24. Moxnes, *Economy of the Kingdom*, p. 129.

25. Batey, *Jesus and the Poor*, p. 21.

26. Theissen, *First Followers*, pp. 38f.; Wolfgang Stegemann, *The Gospel and the Poor* (Philadelphia: Fortress, 1981), p. 52.

27. Grant, "St. Mark," p. 852.

Chapter 8

1. Harold W. Hoehner, *Herod Antipas* (Cambridge: Cambridge University Press, 1972; reprint, Grand Rapids: Zondervan, 1980), p. 76; Seán Freyne, *Galilee from Alexander the Great to Hadrian 323 B.C.E. to 135 C.E.* (Notre Dame: University of Notre Dame Press, 1980), pp. 191f.

2. The Gospel of Matthew substitues the name "Matthew" for "Levi" in Matt. 9:9. In Matt. 10:3, Matthew is called a "tax collector." See S. MacLean Gilmour, "The Gospel According to St. Luke," *The Interpreter's Bible* (New York: Abingdon, 1952), 8:108.

3. Seán Freyne, *Galilee, Jesus and the Gospels* (Philadelphia: Fortress, 1988), p. 54.

4. Gerd Theissen, *The First Followers of Jesus* (London: SCM, 1978), p. 86.

5. Hoehner, *Herod Antipas*, p. 77; Freyne, *Galilee, Jesus and the Gospels*, p. 147.

6. Jack P. Lewis, *The Gospel According to Matthew* (Austin, Tex.: Sweet, 1976), 2:58; Halvor Moxnes, *The Economy of the Kingdom* (Philadelphia: Fortress, 1988), p. 54.

7. Gilmour, "St. Luke," p. 108.

8. John R. Donahue, "Tax Collectors and Sinners," *Catholic Biblical Quarterly* 33 (January 1971): 45.

9. Joachim Jeremias, *Jerusalem in the Time of Jesus* (Philadelphia: Fortress, 1969), pp. 124–26.

10. Hoehner, *Herod Antipas*, p. 76. Also see the map of chief trade routes in Seán Freyne's *Galilee from Alexander the Great to Hadrian 323 B.C.E. to 135 C.E.* (Notre Dame: University of Notre Dame Press, 1980), p. xvii; J. Andrew Overman, "Who Were the First Urban Christians?" *Society of Biblical Literature 1988 Seminar Papers* (Atlanta: Scholars, 1988), p. 161.

11. Theissen, *First Followers*, pp. 41–45.

12. Ibid., p. 43; Freyne, *Galilee from Alexander the Great*, p. 200.

13. Hoehner, *Herod Antipas*, p. 75; Freyne, *Galilee from Alexander the Great*, p. 191; Donahue, "Tax Collectors and Sinners," p. 48.

14. Freyne, *Galilee from Alexander the Great*, pp. 191f.

15. Josephus, *Jewish War* 2.111; *Jewish Antiquities* 17.342–44.

16. Hoehner, *Herod Antipas*, p. 76.

17. Josephus, *Jewish Antiquities* 17.205; 18.90.

18. Ibid., 18.149f.

19. Yacakov Meshorer, "The Lead Weight," *Biblical Archaeologist* 49 (March 1986): 16f.

20. Josephus, *Jewish War* 2.95; *Jewish Antiquities* 17.318.

21. Ibid., 18.250–52; *Life* 36–39.

22. Gilmour, "St. Luke," p. 140: "One group wishes to play 'weddings,' the other 'funerals,' and neither proposal is mutually acceptable. The parable reflects the discouragement that Jesus often experienced in his ministry, but he lightens it with a touch of humor." See also Joachim Jeremias, *The Parables of Jesus* (New York: Charles Scribner's Sons, 1963), pp. 160–62; Günther Bornkamm, *Jesus of Nazareth* (New York: Harper, 1960), p. 50.

23. Jeremias, *Parables of Jesus*, pp. 132–34; Theissen, *First Followers*, p. 105; John R. Donahue, *The Gospel in Parable* (Philadelphia: Fortress, 1988), pp. 147–49.

24. Jeremias, *Parables of Jesus*, pp. 134–36; Donahue, *Gospel in Parable*, pp. 149–51.

25. Pheme Perkins, *Hearing the Parables of Jesus* (New York: Paulist, 1981), p. 173; Eta Linnemann, *Jesus of the Parables* (New York: Harper & Row, 1966), pp. 80f.; C. H. Dodd, *The Parables of the Kingdom* (London: Nisbet, 1936), p. 120.

26. Hoehner, *Herod Antipas*, p. 78; Theissen, *First Followers*, p. 45; Freyne, *Galilee, Jesus and the Gospels*, p. 95.

27. Donaue, *Gospel in Parable*, pp. 187–91; Jeremias, *Parables of Jesus*, pp. 139–44.

28. Perkins, *Hearing the Parables of Jesus*, pp. 171f.

29. Lewis, *Matthew*, 2:99–102.

30. Josephus, *Jewish War* 2.118.

31. F. C. Grant, "The Gospel According to St. Mark," *The Interpreter's Bible* (New York: Abingdon, 1951), 7:841.

32. Lewis, *Matthew*, 2:101.

33. Bornkamm, *Jesus of Nazareth*, pp. 122f.; Joachim Jeremias, *Rediscovering the Parables* (New York: Charles Scribner's Sons, 1966), pp. 111–15.

Chapter 9

1. Kaari Ward, ed., *Jesus and His Times* (Pleasantville: Reader's Digest, 1987), pp. 129–34.

2. Ibid., p. 137.

3. Ibid., pp. 138–44.

4. See Seán Freyne, *Galilee from Alexander the Great to Hadrian 323 B.C.E. to 135 C.E.* (Notre Dame: University of Notre Dame Press, 1980), pp. 126, 128; Stuart Saul Miller, *Studies in the History and Traditions of Sepphoris* (Ann Arbor: University Microfilms International, 1983), pp. 65–70, 72–75.

5. Josephus, *Jewish Antiquities* 17.164–67; Miller, *Studies*, pp. 141–49.

6. Freyne, *Galilee from Alexander the Great*, p. 126. See also nn.60–61 on p. 149.

7. Jack P. Lewis, *The Gospel According to Matthew* (Austin, Tex.: Sweet, 1976), 2:87.

8. Ward, *Jesus and His Times*, pp. 133, 137.

9. John H. Hayes, *Introduction to the Bible* (Philadelphia: Westminster, 1971), p. 361: "Without any doubt, it was this attack on the Temple more than anything else that eventually resulted in the execution of Jesus (Mark 11:18)."

10. Nahman Avigad, *Discovering Jerusalem* (New York: Thomas Nelson, 1980), p. 95.

11. Ibid., p. 99.

12. Ibid., p. 120.

13. Josephus, *Jewish War* 2.169–74; *Jewish Antiquities* 18.55–59.

14. Lewis, *Matthew*, 2:161. Paul L. Maier believes that Jesus' trial before Pilate was in the Citadel, the lavish palace built by Herod the Great near the Jaffa Gate. See *In the Fullness of Time* (New York: Harper-Collins, 1991), pp. 149, 346.

15. Jesus may have carried only the crossbar (*patibulum*). See Ward, *Jesus and His Times*, pp. 257–59.

16. Martin Hengel, *Crucifixion* (Philadelphia: Fortress, 1977), pp. 22–32.

17. Josephus, *Jewish Antiquities* 18.63f. See the reconstruction of this passage based on the tenth-century Agapian manuscript; Paul L. Maier, ed., *Josephus—The Essential Writings* (Grand Rapids: Kregel, 1988), pp. 264f.

18. Thomas R. W. Longstaff, "Nazareth and Sepphoris: Insights into Christian Origins," *Anglican Theological Review* (March 1990): 14f.

Index of Subjects

Index of Scripture

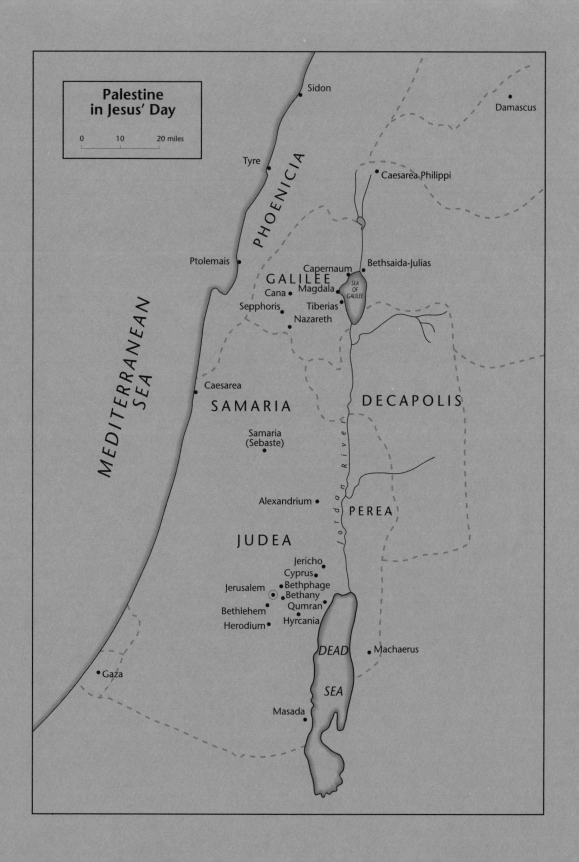

Palestine
in Jesus' Day

0   10   20 miles

Sidon

Damascus

Tyre

PHOENICIA

Caesarea Philippi

Ptolemais

Capernaum   Bethsaida-Julias

GALILEE

Cana   Magdala   SEA OF GALILEE

Sepphoris   Tiberias

Nazareth

MEDITERRANEAN SEA

Caesarea

SAMARIA   DECAPOLIS

Samaria
(Sebaste)

Jordan River

Alexandrium

PEREA

JUDEA

Jericho

Cyprus

Jerusalem   Bethphage
Bethany
Bethlehem   Qumran
Herodium   Hyrcania

DEAD

Machaerus

Gaza

SEA

Masada

The Herodian Genealogy

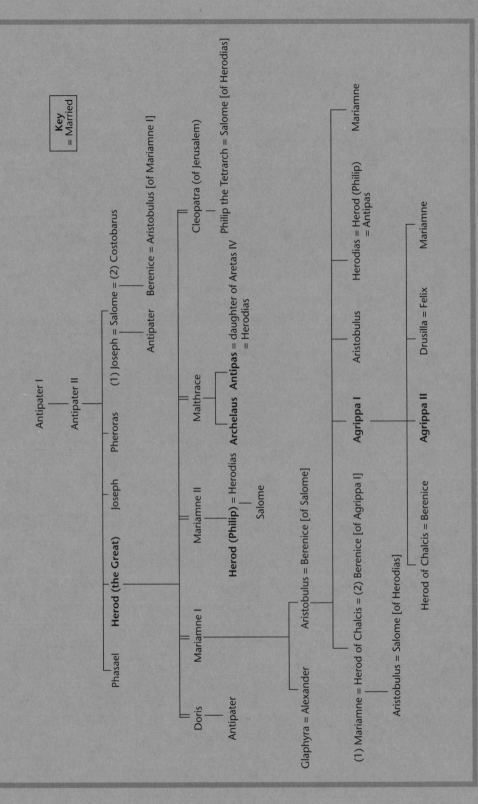

Key
= Married

Antipater I

Antipater II

Phasael   Herod (the Great)   Joseph   Pheroras   (1) Joseph = Salome = (2) Costobarus

Antipater   Berenice = Aristobulus [of Mariamne I]

Cleopatra (of Jerusalem)

Doris   Mariamne I   Mariamne II   Malthrace   Philip the Tetrarch = Salome [of Herodias]

Antipater

Herod (Philip) = Herodias   Archelaus   Antipas = daughter of Aretas IV
= Herodias

Salome

Glaphyra = Alexander   Aristobulus = Berenice [of Salome]

(1) Mariamne = Herod of Chalcis = (2) Berenice [of Agrippa I]   Agrippa I

Aristobulus = Salome [of Herodias]

Herodias = Herod (Philip)
= Antipas

Aristobulus

Mariamne

Herod of Chalcis = Berenice   Agrippa II   Drusilla = Felix   Mariamne